MY PLANET

MY PLANET

FINDING HUMOR IN THE ODDEST PLACES

MARY ROACH

Reader's
digest

The Reader's Digest Association, Inc.
New York, NY / Montreal

A READER'S DIGEST BOOK

Library of Congress Cataloging-in-Publication Data

Roach, Mary.
 My planet : exploring the world with family, friends, and dental floss / Mary Roach.
    pages cm
    ISBN 978-1-62145-071-9 (alk. paper) -- ISBN 978-1-62145-072-6 (epub)
    1. American wit and humor. 2. United States--Social life and customs--Humor. I. Title.
    PN6165.R635 2013
    818'.602--dc23
                        2012044977

We are committed to both the quality of our products and the service we provide to our customers. We value your comments, so please feel free to contact us.

        The Reader's Digest Association, Inc.
        Adult Trade Publishing
        44 South Broadway
        White Plains, NY 10601

For more Reader's Digest products and information, visit our website:
        www.rd.com (in the United States)
        www.readersdigest.ca (in Canada)

Printed in the U.S.A.

7 9 10 8 6

Contents

Introduction

To describe iconic American author Mary Roach is to understand the most genius of Dr. Jekyll and Mr. Hyde complexes. Take science and imbue it with sarcasm. Create a social commentary and add sentimentality. Detail death and layer on wit. Are you chuckling while reading a story about a funeral? Then you're doing exactly what Roach intended. She lifted the gauze on mortality with *Stiff: The Curious Lives of Human Cadavers*, questioned life after death in *Spook: Science Tackles the Afterlife*, experimented with love and the lab for the sake of *Bonk: The Curious Coupling of Science and Sex*, and dove into disturbing aspects of space travel in *Packing for Mars: The Curious Science of Life in the Void*.

While her books focus on science and the supernatural, Roach's column in Reader's Digest zeroed in on the wonders of the everyday. When "My Planet" first appeared in our July 2002 issue, we knew that we had something special. As an institution that prides itself in handpicking moving stories that will make you smile and see the world a little bit differently, we were thrilled to add a writer with both abilities to our treasure trove of authors. Editors eagerly flipped to Roach's column after receiving their first-bound copies of the issue and readers, too, took notice. Three years after it's debut, Roach's column was runner-up in the humor category of the National Press Club awards. Here, you can read her entire collection in one laugh-out-loud volume.

What you can expect from Roach is a curious curation and condensation of life's little mishaps—all of which are filigreed with her humor. She details first dates, rants about marital differences, and dissects (as she is wont to do) the stellar process that is getting older (or, as Roach puts it, entering "the Age of Skirted Swimwear"). She breaks down her hypochondriac tendencies and divulges her uncanny desire to make lists for absolutely everything. In lieu of the latter, here are a few more things she'll tell you about: Accompanying spouses to container outlets ("These stores cast a spell on people"), theories on compromising ("Like any normal couple, we refused to accept each other's differences and did whatever we could to annoy the other person"), and the trials and tribulations of real estate ("The other day—true story—we saw a listing that said 'yard, complete with outhouse'"). Serving as the nucleus to these funny anecdotes is her husband, Ed, who makes appearances as both a funny adversary and a worthy teammate.

In a piece called "Best Cheap Fun!" Roach details free ways to get the most out of life. The list (of course it's a list) includes rooting for the Red Sox at Yankee Stadium and trying to sneak a bottle of water onto a plane, proving once again that humor is worth a potential black eye. Beyond that, Roach prompts us to find wonder in the smaller, simpler moments, leading us to a reader's paradise of which we'll never tire.

—The Editors of Reader's Digest

Soap Opera

It was our first date together. The man who was to become my husband, the man I call Ed, got up from the table within minutes of his arrival and excused himself to go wash his hands. I found this adorable. He was like a little raccoon, leaning over the stream to tidy himself before eating. At the same time I found it odd, as it typically would not occur to me to wash my own hands before a meal, unless I'd spent the afternoon coal mining, say, or running an offset printing press.

It was at this same dinner that I made the unfortunate decision to share my philosophy of bath towels, which holds that you needn't wash them very often because you're clean when you use them.

We both sensed something of a hygiene gap, and, not wanting to alarm one another, spent our first six months trying to hide our true selves. Ed didn't tell me how he'd replace the toilet seat whenever he moved into a new place, on the grounds that he "didn't know who'd been sitting on it." He said nothing when I used the Designated Countertop Sponge to wash the dishes and the Designated Dishwashing Sponge to clean the bathtub, an act I now know to be tantamount to a bioterror attack. For my part, when I dropped food on the floor I'd throw it away instead of picking it up and eating it, and I'd clean the spot where it landed, albeit with the wrong sponge.

As time went by, we reverted to our true selves and the Hygiene War commenced. More than anything else, it was a war of perception. Ed has crud vision, and I don't. I don't notice filth. Ed sees it everywhere. I am reasonably convinced that Ed can actually *see* bacteria. Like any normal couple, we refused to accept each other's differences and did whatever we could to annoy the other person. I flossed my teeth in bed and drank from the OJ container. Ed insisted on moving our vitamins out of the bathroom and into the kitchen, where the germs are apparently less savage. He confessed he didn't like me using his bathrobe because I'd wear it while sitting on the toilet.

"It's not like it goes in the water," I protested, though if you counted the sash as part of the robe, this wasn't strictly true.

"Doesn't matter," Ed said. Ed has a theory that anything that touches the toilet, even the top of the closed lid—which I pretty much use as a dressing table in the mornings—is unclean and subject to the sanitary laws of Leviticus.

Things came to a head one evening at a local eatery.

When Ed returned to the table after washing his hands, I told him there was no rational reason to do that unless he was planning to handle his food and then leave it sitting out at room temperature for three or four hours before eating it. This reminded me of something I had recently learned in the course of my work, which was *not even raccoons wash up before eating.* Yes, according to wildlife expert David Mc-Cullough, of Wartburg College in Waverly, Iowa, raccoons are not washing, but merely handling their food. They do it even when there's no water around. "It's a tactile thing," he told me. "They have extremely sensitive hands, and one idea is that they are just fulfilling a need to feel food moving around in their paws."

I told this to Ed. He looked like he wanted to strangle me, and Professor McCullough too. I followed his gaze to the true source of his emotion: the restaurant's cook. The man had his right hand tucked in his left armpit and was absently massaging the flesh as he read our dinner order and prepared to contaminate Ed's halibut.

"Big deal," I said. "He's wearing a shirt. Maybe he has extremely sensitive hands and it fulfills a need."

Ed called me insane. I called him abnormal. He was right, I was right. We decided we canceled each other out and that together we made one sane, normal entity, at least compared to, I don't know, raccoons. Then Ed did something very touching. He reached over and kissed my hand, which we both knew hadn't been washed since the night before.

To Do *or* Not to Do

There are three kinds of people in this world: 1) People who make lists, 2) People who don't make lists, and 3) People who carve tiny Nativity scenes out of pecan hulls. I'm sorry, there isn't really a third category; it's just that a workable list needs a minimum of three items, I feel. I am, as you might have guessed, a person who makes lists: daily To Do lists, long-term To Do lists, shopping lists, packing lists. I am married to a man whose idea of a list is a corner torn off a newspaper page, covered with words too hastily written to later decipher, and soon misplaced or dropped on the floor. Every now and then I'll discover one of Ed's lists in some forgotten corner of the house: *Rescrangen polfiter,* it will say. Pick up *grellion. Bregoo!* underlined twice.

It isn't entirely accurate to say that Ed has no formal To Do list. He does. It's just that it isn't Ed that makes it, it's me. It's easy enough, as the same 10 or 12 items, mostly involving home-repair projects abandoned midterm, have been on it for years. I once wrote it out for him and put it on the side of the fridge. When I glanced at it some months later, nothing had been crossed off, though he'd added a few of his own: *Make violin. Cure diabetes. Split atom.*

I make lists to keep my anxiety level down. If I write down 15 things to be done, I lose that vague, nagging sense that there are an overwhelming number of things to be done, all of which are on the brink of being forgotten. Ed, on the other hand, controls his anxiety precisely by forgetting them. If they're not there on some numbered piece of paper, they don't exist. So there's no reason why he shouldn't come directly home and turn on the game. People like me really gum up the works for people like Ed by calling them during the day to see if they've gotten around to any of the things on the To Do list we're secretly keeping for them.

Here's the sick thing: I don't really care whether Ed has done the things on this list. I just want to be able to cross them off. My friend Jeff best summed up the joy of crossing off: "No matter how unproductive my week has been, I have a sense of accomplishment." Jeff actually tried to convince me that the adjective *listless* derived from the literal definition "having no lists."

It is possible, I'll admit, to go overboard. Ed once caught me crossing an errand off my list—just for the satisfaction. I have a list of party guests in my desk drawer that dates from around 1997. Every so often I take it out and add the people we've met, cross off the couples that have moved away, and then put it back in my drawer. I long ago came to accept that we're never actually going to have this party; we're just going to keep updating the list—which, for people like me, is a party all by itself.

My husband is the first person I ever met who doesn't even make a shopping list. Ed prefers to go up and down all the aisles, figuring he'll see all the things we need. The problem is that he has no idea whether we actually need them that week, and so it is that we have six cans of water chestnuts and enough Tabasco sauce to sober up the population of Patoka, Indiana, on any given New Year's Day. It seems to be a male pride thing. "Men don't want to admit that they can't remember everything," says my friend Ron. It's the same reason, he says, that men carry their groceries in their arms: "We're too proud to use a cart." Ron finds shopping lists limiting. "Take M&M's," he says. "Those are never going to be on the list."

Ed agrees. He says the things on lists are always chores and downers. Ed wants a To Do list that says, 1) Giants game, 2) Nap, 3) Try new cheese-steak place. Meanwhile, the *polfiter* sits *unscrangened*.

42 Minutes and Holding . . .

Thank you for calling VeriCom Customer Care. Your call is important to us, though not as important as it is to you. If you are calling from a touch-tone phone, press or say 1. If you are calling from a rotary-dial phone, please stay on the line while a customer-care representative makes mocking, derisive faces. Para assistencia en español, go to South America and try your call again.

Your call may be monitored and/or recorded for staff entertainment purposes. For security reasons, please enter the last four digits of your junior high school locker combination, followed by your mother's pet name for your father on evenings when she's had too much sherry.

To save us money and expedite the dismissal of customer-care representatives, our express automated-speech response system is now available. To use this system, press 1. To speak to a customer-care representative, call the Peterson County unemployment office. To hear these options again, hang up and call back.

Welcome to the express automated-speech response system. Please say your 67-digit personal account number, located on the upper lower left middle corner of the one page of your bill that has gone missing, followed by the pound sign. If you thought * was the pound sign, say Ding Dong.

I heard: 894375904279643850432759478847686350542356889448590824837698072459. If this is correct, say Yes. If this is not correct, it's your fault. You are mumbling, or have a funny accent.

For payment information, say Payment. If you have calls and charges you don't understand, say Pinhead. To hear these options again, say Attention Span of a Gnat. To hear the call of the long-toed stint, say kirrrrr-PIP! wacka wacka wacka!

Welcome to the automated payment information center. Our records show a payment of $149 was posted on January 23, 2002, following a 12-day processing period, during which time Accounts Receivable Clerk June Smetak was unaccountably absent and consequently your payment was recorded six days after the due date. A late fee of as much as we can possibly charge without government intervention has been posted to your account. Accounts Receivable Clerk Smetak has been promoted. Whoever said life was fair?

To exit the express automated-speech response system, press or say 1. To enter your 67-digit personal account number again for no special reason, press or say 2.

Please wait, a customer-care representative will be with you shortly, or be short with you, or something. Currently all of our representatives are busy helping dilute our profits. Calls will be answered in the order in which we feel like. Your expected wait time is 42 minutes. Your expected blood pressure is 210/130. You may hear clicks followed by silence. You may hear "Whole Lotta Love" done entirely in strings. You may hear yourself say regrettable things, which may be monitored and/or recorded.

For example, our records show that you used the phrase "gabbling nitwit" during your last call to customer care. This has been noted in your record and will be reflected in the quality of service you receive and the tone of voice of the customer-care representative, should you somehow manage to reach one.

I'm sorry, 0 is not a valid prompt, even if pushed furiously 11 times in rapid succession.

To use our express automated-speech response system, press 1. To hear our website address, press 2. To speak to someone about your anger-management problem, press 3.

Three is not a valid prompt. Thank you for calling.

The Way I Can't See It

This is a story of loss and denial. It begins in Colorado, on the freeway. I am looking for an exit called Drake Way. I notice I am hunched forward, squinting, barely going 40. All around me, drivers beam hate rays into my car. At precisely the moment at which it is too late to veer out of the exit lane, I note that the sign above me does not say Drake Way; it says Homer P. Gravenstein Memorial Highway. This is not good.

I go to my optometrist, who hesitates to up my prescription. She says that with a stronger distance correction, I'm going to start having trouble with what she calls "close work." Apparently she has mistaken me for one of her patients who assemble microchips or tat antimacassars by firelight. I tell her she should go ahead and change the prescription because I don't do close work.

"Do you look things up in phone books?" she asks. "Use maps?" She means, Do I read small print? She means I'm going to have trouble with small print. That I'm suddenly, without warning, old and enfeebled. Nonsense, I insist.

She shrugs and gives me a pair of stronger lenses to try. Then she hands me a bottle of lens drops, points to the label and asks me to read it. This puzzles me, for any fool can see there's nothing written on that label, just tiny lines of decorative filigree. I study it harder. It *is* writing. "Do not use while operating heavy machinery?" I am guessing. "Now with more real fruit? Homer P. Gravenstein Memorial Highway?" I hang my head. It's time to read the handwriting on the wall, which I can most assuredly do—provided it is neatly spaced and billboard-sized. I am old and my eyesight is going. She says to cheer up, that I don't have to get bifocals, "just a pair of reading glasses." In my book, reading glasses are not cause for cheer. They are cause for depression, or regression, or diphtheria, I don't know exactly, because I can no longer read what's in my book.

There was a time when I wanted to wear half-glasses, the way young children want to have crutches or braces until the day they actually need them. Today I do not want to wear reading glasses, not at all. Reluctantly, I wander over to the local drugstore.

The packaging on the reading glasses shows kindly white-haired people in business suits. The eyeglass company has gone out of their way to dress the models like functioning adults, as though people who need reading glasses can still contribute to society, when everyone knows they just sit at home tatting and reading telephone books. I can't go through with it. There has to be another way.

At home, I do an Internet search for "presbyopia." This is a mistake. The websites that turn up have names like SeniorJournal or Friendly4Seniors.com. One site informs me that "presbyopia" comes from the Greek for "elder eye." I don't appreciate this, not one bit. I'm not elderly. I'm 43. Besides, I know some Greek (spanakopita, Onassis, that word you say when the appetizer ignites), and "presbyopia" doesn't sound like any of it. I believe someone made up this "elder eye" business, someone cruel and youthful, with four-point lettering on his business card. I look up the etymology of "presbyopia" in my dictionary, but alas, someone has replaced the words with lines of decorative filigree.

So here's what I'm going to do. I'm not getting bifocals or reading glasses. I'm going to leave my contacts under-corrected and get a pair of distance glasses to wear on top of them, for driving. I figure I've got another five or six years before anyone calls me Elder Eyes. You could say I'm in denial. Or you could write it on a piece of paper, and by God, I'll be able to read it.

Picture Imperfect

The satellite dish was Ed's idea. My husband wanted to be able to watch all 162 Giants games, and for this, he said, he needs a special sports channel. I think what he needs is a special sports therapist, but satellite TV is cheaper, and I gave in. So now, in order for Ed to watch one channel, we'd be paying for 843. I had my work cut out for me.

I sat down with our new baguette-size remote, and pressed On. Right away, Ed began talking, though the TV set sat mute. He explained there were now four separate button-pushes involved in turning on the TV. As he demonstrated, the TV came on. It was a Philippine station, and a man was speaking in Tagalog about his washing machine. "You go Satellite, TV, On, Satellite," Ed was saying. "Get it? For Off, it's Off, TV, Off." I got it the way I get Tagalog washing-machine ads. I muted Ed and called the help line.

"You shouldn't have to push all those buttons," said the Help woman.

I relayed this to Ed, but he didn't hear me, engrossed as he was in *Antiques Roadshow*. A man had lugged in an old museum case of taxidermied birds, no doubt to make room for his new giant remote and satellite receiver, and was showing it to a British chap with a pasted-on smile. "You've got a fantastic array of birds here, don't you?"

I turned back to my pal on the other end of the phone, who was telling me that I was going to have to *reprogram my remote*. This is like being told that in order to shave a few minutes off your walk to work, you were going to have to have your legs removed and sewn on in a new position, which, as it happened, they were doing on the surgery channel at that moment.

Ed eventually found his sports channel. An Indianapolis 500 winner was philosophizing about his career, which racecar drivers maybe shouldn't do: "Sometimes you're the windshield, sometimes the bug."

"Now, to reprogram your remote, you take out the batteries and press the '1' button for 60 seconds," the Help woman—clearly the windshield here—was saying. "Then put the batteries back and hold down the 'TV' button at the same time as you enter the TV brand code, which you can look up in your manual." It was going to require six arms, minimum, which the surgeons of Channel 89 could no doubt arrange.

I became intrigued with a button labeled *Fetch,* no doubt the source of many a humorous exchange between remote-holding, sandwich-wanting husbands and their wives. The feature would allow Ed to input a keyword, such

14

as "Giants," or "baseball," or "big, fat waste of time" and, with the press of a button (or 18 buttons), fetch channels that matched. Ed entered "Giants," and the TV reported that they were appearing on Channel 573. He pressed Fetch. The TV gamely fetched a blank channel.

As it turns out, we only get about 225 of 843 channels, the rest appearing as blank screens, requiring the viewer to scroll endlessly—effectively ruining the all-American channel-surfing experience.

I called the Help woman back, demanding to know how to get rid of the blank stations. She asked if I'd looked in my User's Guide. I didn't like where this was heading. If I wanted to read and exercise comprehension skills, I wouldn't be watching television.

In no time at all, though, I was surfing gleefully. I had wanted to hate satellite TV, but it's so wonderfully, derangedly entertaining. Here was Barney Rubble ordering chopped pterodactyl livers. Here was the incredible Flat Hose, attaching easily to any faucet!

There was Gene Rayburn on the Game Show Channel, introducing a contestant with "a hobby of opera and swimming," which one dearly hopes are not practiced simultaneously. I smiled to myself, like the British chap from *Antiques Roadshow.* "You've got a fantastic array of channels here, don't you?"

Industrial Strength Shopping

When I first met my husband, I did not know about price clubs. I simply thought I was dating a man for whom it was very important never to run out of things. Ed owned entire shrink-wrapped bricks of canned tuna, though by all outward appearances he was not a man passionate about tuna fish. For as long as I'd known him, there was a 500-count box of latex gloves in the closet. He had eight orange plastic-handled pairs of scissors and six glue sticks. I began to think he had run a kindergarten out of his home and that when it was closed down—no doubt owing to parental discomfort over the rubber gloves—he was left with the classroom and lunch supplies.

Then one bold shining day, Ed took me by the hand and brought me to Costco. Initially I was aghast. Who were these poor people who could use up to 112 packets of Alka-

Seltzer or a 2-pack of jumbo-sized bottles of Immodium in a single lifetime? Then we hit the food aisles, and I understood who they were. They were the people eating 18-packs of Vienna sausages and 6-pound cans of garbanzo beans in a single lifetime. I began to see the place as a vast conspiracy of bigness, one colossal, insane purchase leading to another. Need a bigger refrigerator for your 30-pound salmon? Aisle 11. Need a 10-pound box of Arm & Hammer to freshen up that big refrigerator? Aisle 5. If you're buying 72 frankfurters, better get the gallon tub of French's.

"Two seventy-nine," said Ed, of the French's, looking rapt. "You can't afford not to buy this mustard." It's a sickness, and my husband is well beyond help.

Next to the entrancing mustard was a white plastic bucket of mayonnaise, looking like it had taken a wrong turn on the way to The Home Depot. The soy sauce came in a metal one-gallon can of the sort used to transport gas to your car when you've been running on empty, as you tend to do when your bank account has been drained dry by army-sized requisitions of cling peaches and Dimetapp. What happened to bottles you can actually fit into your kitchen? Is it worth saving $1.71 if it means spooning condiments from industrial vats into more manageably sized bottles, thereby soiling countless shirts with spots that will not come out even with 406 applications of SHOUT?

Then there's the fact that Ed is one of those guys who likes to walk down all the aisles when they shop. At a place as vast as Costco, you don't enter into this lightly. You need good arch support and a map, possibly a donkey and canteen. To get out in under an hour, you'll need to break into a jog. Given you are about to buy snack foods totaling 350,000,000 calories, jogging's probably a good idea, but still and all . . .

"Perfect," said Ed when I pointed out how long it would take. He'd dropped off film at the Costco one-hour developers. "Go try on some glasses at Costco Optical," he said when I complained. "Go watch the TVs. Sample a sausage." Gradually, I succumbed. Now we pretty much live at Costco. It's working out nicely, as our home is a warehouse for paper towels and mustard and giant flats of beverages.

My fondness for the place continued to blossom until one day the kindly man at Hector's, my neighborhood office supply store, complained about all the business he was losing to places like Costco and OfficeMax. Some weeks later, while stocking up on office supplies at Costco, I felt a twinge of guilt. It was a small twinge, and somewhat hard to detect what with the giddiness of finding printer cartridges for half the price I was paying at Hector's, but I was torn.

Then I saw something horrifying. I nudged Ed and pointed to a man cutting up sample-sized bites of string cheese with a pair of scissors. Something about him looked familiar, though perhaps it was just the orange-handled scissors and the latex gloves. "Is that Hector?" I whispered to Ed. I wondered aloud whether all the people who owned the grocery stores and office supply shops driven out of business were now standing around in hairnets, working at Costco. Ed nodded thoughtfully and put a Mega-Bag of Fun-Sized candy bars in the cart, on the grounds that Halloween was just around the corner. (It was March.)

That night, sensing rebellion, Ed sat down with one of our three identical calculators (for those times when three family members need to work out complex math problems simultaneously) and totted up our annual savings due to Costco. On beer alone, it was over $50. I tried to argue that you had to subtract the money spent on food items sitting uneaten for over two years, such as the two-foot-by-one-foot carton of chicken teriyaki strips currently serving as a sort of display platform for ice cubes and Popsicles in our freezer. Ed countered that keeping a large, frozen object in the freezer made it more efficient and cut down on electric bills. There was no fighting it. Costco rules the universe (and is slightly bigger).

Meet the Parents

My mother had a saying: "Guests are like fish. After three days they begin to stink." Here's the thing about my mother, though. She never bought fresh fish. She bought Mrs. Paul's frozen fish sticks, which she served us every Friday along with Tater Tots, leading me to think that good Catholics ate golden-brown food on Fridays. Here's the other thing about my mother. She never had guests. Only once in my childhood did someone from her or my father's family stay overnight at our house. In my father's case, it was because his family lived in England, and he'd lost touch with them. In my mother's case, who knows. Possibly it was her cooking.

I'm guessing the fish line must have been something her own mother said.

I wouldn't know, because I only met my grandmother once. When I was five, we took the train out to Walla Walla to visit my mother's family for the first and last time. I can't remember any interaction with Grandma, or even if that was what we called her. I remember that Uncle Al had a farm with a hayloft to play in, and ripe strawberries we could pick and eat until our bellies were bursting.

I know Uncle George had a red-haired daughter named Cacky, whom I adored, and that Aunt Louise scolded my brother and me for winding up the chains on the swing set and spinning ourselves dizzy. And that's it: the sum total of my memories of my parents' relatives. To this day, my family in Washington are strangers to me.

My husband's mother also has a saying: "We love you. When are we going to see you again?" Ed's family—his parents and his sister and her husband and little girl—come out to stay with us, or us with them, three or more times a year. When they come to town, they all pile into our home, and when we go to Florida, we all pile into theirs. Neither place has a guest room, but both have sofas and floors, and that's enough. The first time we came to visit, Ed's parents insisted on giving us their bed. His dad slept on the couch and his mom took the love seat. We thought the love seat was a pullout sofa bed, but in the morning we found her with her legs hanging over the arm. If anything could stink after three days, you'd think that would, but as always, Jeanne couldn't bear to see us go.

Of course, I know what my mother meant. For the first three days of a visit, you are caught up in the joy and novelty of seeing one another. You're busy catching up. It doesn't bother you that you have no time to yourself, that you have to wait to use the shower and have to drink coffee that's not made the way you like it. From day four onward, there's a subtle shift. You're running out of news to talk over and outings to pass the time and meals that everyone can happily eat. Patience begins to fray. By day six, something as trivial as a coffee table water ring can seem like grounds for a NATO tribunal. You begin to view your guests through the magnifying glasses of the put-upon host. A TV set turned four decibels higher than you like registers as "blaring." Making a 13-cent long-distance call is perceived as "running up my phone bill!"

Ed's family often stays six or seven days. By the last day, I admit I'm ready to have my home back to normal, to get dressed in the room where my clothes live. Six rooms aren't enough for five guests, but I blame the apartment for my feelings, not the guests. I don't want them to go after three days, I just want the building to get larger.

I've come to love Ed's relatives. I think of them as family in a way that I never thought of my own relatives in Walla Walla—that collection of names and faces on Christmas cards. And I couldn't have these feelings about Ed's family if they didn't come visit as often as they do, or if they stayed in a hotel and dropped by for meals. Family are people who live together—if only for a week at a time. They're people who drop towels on your bathroom floor, put your cups and glasses back in the wrong place and complain about your weather. You do it to them, they do it to you, and none of you would have it any other way.

She's Got Game

On any given night for the 14 or so months of the year corresponding to baseball season, our TV is likely to be tuned to a sports channel. In order to maintain some semblance of personal contact with my husband, Ed, during these months, I often sit beside him on the couch with a book. I don't mind the chatter of the sportscasters, for my brain processes sports talk in the same way it processes paid political announcements and the cell-phone conversations of strangers.

A man in a navy blazer will say, "No atta-babies in that at-bat!" and his companion will chime in with, "It was right there, in the whack-me zone!" and it's as though they're not there.

Sometimes I find myself staring at the game anyway. I watch sports the way a dog will watch TV: I'm attracted by the motion and color, but no actual comprehension is taking place. Ed forgets that this is the case. He'll see me looking at the screen and assume I'm following the game and expect me to keep track of what happens while he goes to the kitchen for a refreshing beverage. Sometimes I'm able to bluff my way through it ("He had it right there in the whack-me zone, honey!"), but more often I am forced to confess that I have not grasped the significance of anything I have seen.

This is where it gets ugly. This is where Ed tries to turn his wife into—as the men in the blazers like to say—a serious student of the game. Plainly put, this cannot be done. You'd have more luck getting a pug to understand *Jeopardy!* Take, for instance, the Infield Fly Rule, which begins, in the breezy parlance of the Official Baseball Rules, like this: "The batter is out when it is declared, and the ball does not have to be caught. Because the batter is declared out, the runners are no longer forced to run, but they can run if they wish, at the risk of being put out . . ."

"What?" Ed will ask. "What don't you get?" Apparently this language speaks to him in a way that it does not speak to me. One night I decided to try putting it to work. It was seven o'clock and cutlets were growing cold. I cleared my throat. "The wife is declared put out when it is dinnertime and the game is still running. The husband's attention has to be caught and because the wife is put out, the husband may wish to run . . ."

Ed begged leniency on the grounds that it was "the top of the ninth." Here again, communication breaks down. For me, there can be no understanding of a sport where the "top" of an inning is the first half. "Think of ladders," I said, as Marvin Benard stepped up to the plate. "You start at the bottom and go to the top." But Ed wasn't listening.

Benard struck out, and Ed said hurtful things about him. This is my other qualm with pro sports. I feel bad for the players when they mess up. The ball Benard missed was going 90 m.p.h., and it went all crooked. If I were the umpire, I would have laid a hand on the man's shoulder and said, "Take your base, Marv. You were really close."

Last October my tolerance for Ed's devotion to sports, already threadbare, began to unravel. The baseball season was winding down, leading me to think that we could resume our normal adult activities, if only we had any. I came into the living room one Sunday to find Ed, a man who dismisses football as "a bore," engrossed in a Broncos game. He wore a guilty grin. "Third and long, sweetie!"

It was around that time that I came across a book about sports "addiction." It said that for many men, their relationship with their team fulfills a need for intimacy. This got me right there in the whack-me zone. Was J. T. Snow doing more for my husband than I was?

I confronted Ed. There was an NFL game on that day, but he wasn't watching. He was making banana bread. Though he denied the charges, he wouldn't rule out the possibility that J. T. Snow could make him happy. Then he asked if I wanted to go for a bike ride. I decided to drop the sports addiction thing, because truly, Ed doesn't deserve the hassle. He's the winningest guy I know, and I mean that from the bottom of my heart, which is the part that comes before the top.

Don't Bring Me Flowers

Some years ago, a well-known perfume company invented a concept called "the Aviance night." In the ads, a housewife was shown primping for a night on the town, sashaying around the bedroom and flipping her hair from one side to the other as she puts on her earrings. As she douses herself with Aviance perfume, an unseen chorus conjectures excitedly that "she's gonna have an Aviance night!"

I never had an Aviance night. I don't, as a general rule, sashay. But I cannot completely silence that part of me that longs, every now and again, to be heading off confidently and aromatically into a night of candlelit romance. My longing tends to coalesce and rise to the surface, like chicken fat, every February.

A word about Valentine's Day. This was originally a holiday for a god who protected shepherds' flocks from the wolves outside Rome. I don't know how we got from livestock surveillance to romantic love, but if I had to tender a guess I'd say it had something to do with the Hallmark company. We really have to watch these guys, because soon we're going to find ourselves sending cards for Plumbers and Steamfitters Day ("You bring a special kind of caring to our water-serviced area . . .").

It's not that my husband and I don't go out. Every Valentine's Day, Ed will dutifully reserve a table at a romantic restaurant. I look forward to it until about five o'clock on the actual date. Somehow the mood never seems to fit. I put on perfume and wait for the unseen chorus to kick in, but hear instead the dulcet tones of my sweatpants calling out to me. Suddenly I don't feel like going to an unfamiliar, overpriced restaurant. I want to go somewhere comfortable and known, a place where the wine doesn't cost more than my shoes and the waiter won't look down upon me for making "daikon" rhyme with "bacon."

But this is Valentine's Day, and we must persevere. For tomorrow, the Aviance Day After, friends and coworkers will grill us as to the activities of the night before. "The living room" is not an acceptable answer to "Where did Ed take you for Valentine's?"

This year is no different. Poor Ed. He's trying very hard. As we dress to leave, he takes my hands in his and leans in close. He cocks his head to one side, as if seeing me anew, in the fresh dawn of reawakened love. "Are you wearing an odor?"

Ed is romantic, but not in the traditional manner. I

once suggested that we bring the dining room candles into the bedroom. Ed brought them in and set them down on the floor near the door, at the farthest point from the bedspread and other combustibles, completely out of our view. "They still provide some nice ambient illumination," he said. It was like getting into bed with Norm Abram.

I once asked him to pick up some massage oil, and he came home with an unscented variety. I didn't know such a thing existed. Another time he tried to surprise me with a romantic bubble bath, not realizing that sometime during the day, something had gone wrong with the hot water heater, and the bath water was stone cold. No doubt we'd forgotten to send flowers on Plumbers and Steamfitters Day and the Local 486 had sabotaged our tank.

The Valentine's Day dinner itself is always a bit of a trial. From the moment you're seated, the gazing and hand-holding must begin. Everyone else is doing it, and so you must too. No matter what kind of day you've had or how long you've been married, the two of you must appear to be utterly, helplessly captivated by each other, unable to think about anything else. This does not work, for one simple, incontrovertible reason. A man at a restaurant table is thinking about food. He cannot help himself. He knows this isn't allowed and will try very, very hard to appear to be thinking thoughts of love. The effort typically fails, and he achieves a look somewhere between hypnosis and acid reflux.

I say Valentine's Day should have term limits. I say

if you're old enough to have trouble reading a menu by candlelight, you're old enough that you shouldn't have to bother. Kiss each other across a plate of spaghetti, while an unseen chorus admits that the Aviance night was always a little overrated.

Roomba's Revenge

I have always wanted and not wanted a cleaning person. On the one hand, I want very much for someone else to clean our house, as neither I nor my husband, Ed, has shown any aptitude for it. On the other hand, I'd feel guilty inflicting such distasteful drudgery on another human being. No one but me, for instance, should have to clean up the dental floss heaped like spaghetti near the wastebasket where I toss it each night, never catching on that floss is not something that can be thrown with a high degree of accuracy.

You can imagine my joy upon reading that the iRobot company of Somerville, Massachusetts, has invented a robotic vacuum. They call it Roomba. Their website plays an animated clip of what appears to be an enlarged CD Walkman scooting across a living room carpet, sucking up conspicuous chunks of unidentified detritus. Meanwhile, sentences run across the screen: "I'm having lunch with a friend" . . . "I'm planting flowers in the garden." The point is that you can go out and "enjoy life" while your robot cleans up the conspicuous chunks strewn about your living room floor, no doubt rubble tracked in from the garden plot.

Roomba joined our family last week. Right away I changed the name to Reba, in order to indulge my fantasy of having a real cleaning person, yet still respect its incredibly dumb-sounding given name. As techno-gadgets go, the iRobot vacuum is surprisingly simple to use. All you do, beyond switching it on, is tell it the room size. This I calculated in my usual manner, by picturing six-foot guys lying end-to-end along the walls and multiplying accordingly.

I started Reba off in the bedroom. I was on my way out the door to enjoy life, when I heard a crash. My vacuuming robot had tangled itself up in the telephone cord and then headed off in the other direction, pulling the phone off the nightstand and onto the floor. "Maybe Reba needs to make a call," said Ed.

I couldn't, in all fairness, be annoyed, as I'm the sort of person who gets up to go to the bathroom on airplanes without first unplugging my headphones. Only the fact that my head is attached to my neck prevents it from being yanked off onto the floor. Also, it tells you right there in the Owner's Manual to "pick up objects like clothing, loose papers . . . power cords . . . just as you would before using a regular vacuum cleaner."

This poses something of a problem in our house. The corners and the floor space along the walls and under the furniture in the office, for instance, are filled with stacks and bags of what I call Ed's desk runoff. My husband is a man who does not easily throw things away. Whatever he gets in the mail or empties from his pockets he simply deposits on the nearest horizontal surface.

Once a week, like the neighborhood garbage truck, I collect Ed's discards and throw them onto a vast, heaping landfill located on his desk. At a certain point, determined by the angle of the slope and the savagery of my throws, the pile will begin to slide. This is Ed's cue to shovel a portion of it into a shopping bag, which he then puts on the floor somewhere with the intent to go through it later, *later* here meaning "never."

I looked at the floor in our office. There were newspapers, piles of files, socks, pens, not to mention the big guys lying along the floorboards. Picking it all up to clear the way for Reba would take half an hour, which is more time than I normally spend vacuuming. It was the same sort of situation that has kept me from ever hiring an assistant.

It would take longer to explain my filing system to someone else ("Okay, so takeout menus and important contracts go in the orange folder labeled 'Bees' . . .") than it would to do the chore myself.

The bathroom promised to be less problematic. I lifted the hamper into the tub and put the bathroom scale in the sink, where it looked as though maybe it wanted a bath, or maybe it had a date with a vacuum cleaner.

Then I went into the bedroom to fetch Reba, who was at that moment engaged in a shoving match with one of my Birkenstocks. She had pushed the shoe across the room and under the bed, well into the zone of no-reach.

"Good one," said Ed, who has always harbored ill will toward comfort footwear for women.

I set Reba down and aimed her at the crud-paved crawlspace beneath the footed bathtub. I have tried this with Ed and various of my stepdaughters, but it always fails to produce the desired effect.

The wondrous Reba was not only willing but actually enthusiastic about the prospect, motoring full bore across the tile and under the tub and whacking her forehead on the far wall. You just can't find help like that.

The living room was a similar success. Reba does housework much the way I do, busily cleaning in one spot for a while and then wandering off inexplicably in the opposite direction and getting distracted by something else that needs doing. The iRobot people call this an "algorithm-based cleaning pattern," a term I will use the next time Ed catches me polishing silver with the mop water evaporating in the other room.

Halfway across the living room carpet, Reba stopped moving and began emitting undelighted noises. Ed leafed through the troubleshooting guide.

"It's a Whimper Beep," he said, employing the concerned baritone that used to announce the Heartbreak of Psoriasis as though it were the Cuban Missile Crisis. I turned Reba over. Wound around her brushes was a two-foot strand of dental floss. Apparently even robots have their limits.

How I Caught Every Disease on the Web

The Internet is a boon for hypochondriacs like me. Right now, for instance, I'm feeling a shooting pain on the side of my neck. A Web search produces five matches, the first three for a condition called Arnold-Chiari Malformation.

This is the wonderful thing about looking up your symptoms on the Internet. Very quickly you find yourself distracted from your aches and pains. The symptom list for Arnold-Chiari Malformation is three pages long. Noting the four out of 71 symptoms that match, I conclude that I have this condition. A good hypochondriac can make a diagnosis on the basis of one matching symptom.

While my husband, Ed, reads over my shoulder, I recite symptoms from the list. "'General clumsiness' and 'general imbalance,'" I say, as though announcing arrivals at the Marine Corps Ball. "'Difficulty driving,' 'lack of taste,' 'difficulty feeling feet on ground.'"

"Those aren't symptoms," says Ed. "Those are your character flaws."

Ha, ha. But I know how to get back at him. "Hey, what's this thickening, or nodule, on the back of your neck?" Ed is more of a hypochondriac than I am. "Looks like it could be Antley-Bixler Syndrome," I say.

I got this one from the National Organization for Rare Disorders website, which has an index of rare diseases that I've pretty much memorized. I move in for the kill. "Ever feel any fatigue?"

Ed gets on the computer to see if there's a self-test for Antley-Bixler Syndrome. We're big fans of self-tests, and the Internet is full of them. I once happily passed the afternoon self-testing for macular degeneration, emotional eating, hypochondria, bad breath. Ed found me taking the Self-Test for Swine Farm Operators. ("I conduct manure nutrient analysis: Annually. Every five years. Never.") It's probably fair to say that I'm addicted to self-tests, but until there's a self-test for self-test addiction, I can't be sure.

The dangerous thing about Internet diagnosis is that most hypochondriacs will attempt it late at night, when everyone else is asleep and no one is around to reassure them that they're nuts. This is what happened to me on October 2, sometime past midnight, when I entered the words "red spots on my face" into the Google search page. I'd noticed the spots while scanning my face for starlike speckles, an early symptom of Ebola virus.

I ignored the 20 or 30 entries for broken capillaries and

zeroed in on the following: "Leprosy . . . begins with red spots on the face. . . . Bones are affected and fingers drop off." I began to feel panicky and short of breath. I added those symptoms to my search and found this: "I developed little red spots on my face and arms. Then last spring I started becoming short of breath. . . ." Bottom line, I had interstitial lung disease.

I tried to keep calm. I tried to focus on entry No. 18: "Spicy pork rinds cause me to break out in red spots on my face." I couldn't recall eating spicy pork rinds, but perhaps I'd ordered a dish that was made with them but failed to state this on the menu. From now on, I'd be sure to ask. *Waiter, is the flan made with spicy pork rinds?*

In the end, it was no use. I was up all night, fretting over interstitial lung disease. For a hypochondriac, simply running the name of a new disease through your mind once or twice is enough to convince you that you've got it. I frequently remind myself of my stepdaughter Phoebe, who, some years ago, heard someone talking about mad cow disease. The next day when a friend of the family said, "Hi, Phoebe, how are you?" she stated calmly, "I have mad cow disease." But Phoebe was a child. I am an adult. I should know better. Perhaps there's something wrong with me.

TV Dinners

I recently came across a TV show called *The Naked Chef*. You probably all knew this, but the Naked Chef wears clothes. He is no more naked than the Galloping Gourmet was galloping. He's just a British guy cooking.

"They call it that because he uses simple, fresh ingredients—the food's not all gussied up," said my husband, Ed, settling in beside me on the couch.

"Aha." I picked up the remote.

Ed grabbed my wrist. "What are you doing? Emeril's coming up."

Do you recall the look on Mia Farrow's face when she peers into the cradle at the end of *Rosemary's Baby?* Picture that on me. I was about to learn that my husband, watcher of sports and wearer of tool belt, has been checking out the Food Network—daily. Ed works at a newspaper, where they're allowed to have TVs so that they can keep abreast of breaking news, such as Martha Stewart visiting an asparagus farm. Lately, his set has been tuned to the Food Network.

We sat in silence as the Naked Chef made monkfish kebabs. He pronounced the last syllable "babs" not "bobs," and instead of skewers, he was using rosemary sprigs. Adding to the confusion, our chap insisted on giving ingredients in ounces and pints.

"They translate the amounts for you on the recipe you can print out," Ed reassured me while at the same time alarming me deeply, for this meant that he had been visiting the Food Network website. He went and got a Naked Chef pizza dough recipe. "One pint" had been helpfully converted to "568 milliliters." It would be simpler to just move to England.

It took the Naked Chef all of three minutes to ready his kebabs. Here is the seductive deceit of cooking shows. The ingredients have all been washed and diced and set aside in a dozen tiny glass bowls. No one is ever shown tidying up afterward and ruining her manicure washing tiny glass bowls. Ed made an amazing roasted chicken and dumpling soup over the holidays, but because Tyler Florence appeared to make it in 20 minutes, Ed miscalculated, and we ended up eating shortly before midnight. The cleanup brigade is still at it.

I explained this to Ed while the commercials were on. A woman was demonstrating a coffee mug with a built-in blender at the bottom to froth milk so you don't have to buy a milk steamer, but you have to drink out of a blender.

Ed tried to make the point that the shows aren't just

educational, they're entertaining. Unfortunately for him, the network was at that moment broadcasting a segment about whipped dessert-topping strategies. A woman was crowning a piece of pie with a "rippled dollop."

"There is no dark side to this dollop," said the woman, and you couldn't argue with her there.

Emeril was on next. *Emeril Live* is one of the Food Network's most popular shows. It's based on the day-time talk-show format: a sound stage, an excitable studio audience—even a house band. But in place of witty, attractive celebrities and a funny monologue, you get a middle-aged man cooking.

Today Emeril had taken the camera backstage for a tour of his pantry: "Over here we got the snail dishes, the ramekins, the bread pudding cups." Ed and I recently videotaped the contents of our home for insurance purposes. The tape features Ed narrating as the camera pans from one closet shelf to the next: "Extra pillows, place mats. This is a sewing machine . . ." I'm thinking we could use this tape to launch our own entertainment network: the Storage Channel.

Setting aside the issue of whether these shows are entertaining, I raised one final point. The irony, the dark side to this dollop, is that with people watching Emeril three times a day, no one's got time to cook. To prove me wrong, Ed made Food Network crab cakes and broccoli rabe with anchovies. He made them fast, and he made them amazing. I am eating humble pie, only this time I know how to top it in an attractive and professional-looking manner.

Frequent Flierrr#*!

My father-in-law turned 80 this year, and there was a big party in South Florida. A few months beforehand, I decided to use up some frequent flier miles and go. I called United, because they've filed for Chapter 11 and I wanted to get rid of my miles before they get to Chapter 12, which is the chapter where they cut out 70 percent of their routes and start serving Kool-Aid and salami ends.

I gave the frequent flier man the date. There was nothing into Fort Lauderdale, nothing into West Palm Beach. Perhaps it was a blackout date. Frequent Flier Plans, as you know, have more blackout dates than Anna Nicole Smith. It certainly wasn't a holiday, unless you count Bunsen Burner Day. But this hardly merits a blackout.

Bunsen burners may well get the day off, may well wish to go and visit their relatives, but, tragically, FAA regulations prohibit Bunsen burners on airplanes.

There was a flight into Miami, which I said I'd take. I'll

rent a car, I said. I've got lots of those free rental car certificates that the frequent flier programs send you to make you feel better about having to fly into the wrong city on the wrong day. Then again, there's a reason I have lots of these. I can't find anyplace that'll honor one. I'll walk up to the counter and hand the woman my certificate, and she'll start shaking her head. "Today is Wednesday," she'll say slowly and with fraying patience, as though talking to a small driver's-license-bearing child. "This coupon is for the third Friday of a month ending in *E*. It says right here it must be used *before* National Foot Health Day yet *after* the start of the Tule Elk rut season. Besides, we have nothing left but locomotives, and this coupon isn't good for those."

"Oh, one thing," said the United Man. "The Miami flight is on the day before you want to leave. Is that okay? And I see it leaves out of San Jose, not San Francisco. Does that work for you?"

"Sure," I said. "Oh, one thing. My credit card is expired, so I was going to pay you in Betty Crocker coupons. Does that work for you? And I'll be traveling with a family of Bunsen burners. Is that okay?"

The man from United had an idea. He said that if I cashed in 40,000 miles instead of 25,000 miles, there would be more seats available. This would put me in the No Restrictions Category. Unfortunately, it would also put me in the Gave Up a Free Trip to Hawaii Category.

He found me a flight into Fort Lauderdale, and then he said, "There is one stopover. In Chicago." Unless you are trying to draw Anna Nicole Smith with your flight pattern, you don't fly up to Chicago and back down to get to Florida. Clearly we had moved on to Chapter 12. We were right on the brink of Chapter 13, where the CEO sells the company to Air Burundi and you're out of luck unless you happen to be traveling to Bujumbura, and even then you're going to have a plane change in Chicago.

"Okay," I said to the United Man. "Let's say for the sake of argument that I decide to do this. Let's say I trade in my free trip to Hawaii for the opportunity to spend 12 hours with my knees inside a stranger's kidneys, eating embalmed chicken and breathing last year's air. What does the return look like?"

The return looked like an ad for prescription-strength pain reliever. It was one of the busiest days of the year, the man said. All the flights were overbooked. For the Sunday I planned to return was the last day of Spring Break. Spring Break, as you probably know, is a week-long gathering of American college students, similar in many ways to the Tule Elk rut season.

There were no flights at all out of South Florida. I wouldn't be going anywhere with my frequent flier miles, except possibly to my therapist, where there would at least be more legroom.

Hold Everything!

We are in the grip of a nationwide container mania. We have Tupperware and Rubbermaid. There's Hold Everything and a chain called The Container Store. Soon the earth will need a special caddy to organize its container franchises.

This is creating conflict in our home. We don't need conflict in our home, as we've got nowhere to put it. My husband, Ed, is one of those people made nervous by the thought of throwing things away. There may come a day when he'll need bank statements from 1979 and adapters for long-extinct electronics goods. (Everyone saves adapters, thinking they will work on other gadgets—that they're *adaptable*—but this has never happened since the dawn of adapters. Go and throw them away.)

Places like The Container Store only encourage people like Ed. Now they can pretend to be doing something about their clutter. They can put adapters in a special Useless

Adapter Bin. They can organize their junk rather than doing the sensible thing and junking it.

Ed came home from The Container Store last week with a Pull-Out Lid Organizer for all our plastic container lids. Why don't we just get rid of some of our plastic food containers, I said, raining on his parade, as is my wifely wont. At the moment, we've got, oh, 345 of them. But according to the Ed system, you can't throw away perfectly good food. You must put all leftovers in plastic containers until they smell, whereupon you may throw them away, because they're no longer perfectly good food. So it is that our refrigerator does not contain food, but variously sized petri dishes. There's waffle batter in there dating back to the dawn of adapters.

Ed relented on the plastic containers, on one condition: I'd agree to come with him to The Container Store. For he knew what I did not: These stores cast a spell on people. Soon I would be just like him. I'd find myself entranced by a Clear Panty Box, thinking, *Yes, I need to see my undergarments at a glance.* I would catch myself eyeing an acrylic Coffee Filter Holder, thinking, *Handy, attractive, only $8.49.* Were I thinking straight, I would realize that I already own a coffee filter holder, because the filters came in a box, and the box was free.

The last time we were there, Ed fell for an in-closet shoe rack—a good idea, except Ed's shoes rarely make it into a closet. Ed has a near-religious belief in the tidying power of special storage devices. If you buy the rack, the shoes will come.

Half of the first floor of The Container Store is devoted to walk-in closet systems. Thankfully, we have no walk-in closets, so we didn't have to fight about this. Though some people would argue we do have a walk-in closet, and we've chosen to use it as a bedroom. My stepdaughter recently informed us that Mariah Carey's closet is as big as our house. "So our house is the size of a closet?" I said, sounding hurt.

"No." She gave me the implied *duh.* "I mean it's the size of Mariah Carey's closet." The conversation went on in this vein for a while.

I told Ed I expected to get up in the morning and find Mariah Carey wandering forlornly through the dining room in her underwear. He raised a brow. "Wake me, will you?"

Getting back to The Container Store, I had gone away to ponder Gravity-Feed Can Racks, and when I returned, I found Ed by the built-in closet organizers, looking wistful. I could tell he aspired to be the owner of this system, the tidy, color-coordinated man with the wife who wears only suits and pumps. "Where are their sneakers?" I said. "Their sweatshirts? Where's their *stuff?*"

"Besides," I said, "we can't afford to be this organized." One wall of the closet system costs $400. I told Ed I loved him the way he was, with his T-shirts heaped on a chair and his shoes willy-nilly on the rug. I told him I didn't want the dull man with the well-hung tan suits in The Container Store catalog. That no matter how many boxes of bank statements he kept, my love for him would remain as wide and deep as an ocean, or anyway Mariah Carey's closet.

Night Light Fight

If my husband, Ed, had his way, you could pop by our place any given night and see me sitting in bed, struggling to hold my head up under the weight of a night-vision headset. Ed is an early-to-sleep sort of chap, who'll announce around 8 p.m., "Just going to change into my pj's and read for a while." Once he becomes horizontal, however, it's pretty much over.

This makes it difficult for yours truly, for I really *do* read in bed, including the part where you turn the page and read a second one and then a third one. Ed would like for me to do this in a quiet, motionless, pitch-dark manner. Instead, I do it in a chip-crunching, light-on, getting-in-and-out-of-bed-for-more-chips manner. In the spirit of compromise, I bought Ed earplugs and a black satin sleep mask. "It's dashing," I said of the mask. "You look like Antonio Banderas in *Zorro*." This was a lie. He looked like Arlene Francis in "What's My Line?"

"Zorro didn't wear a sleep mask," countered Ed. "His had eyeholes cut out."

"It was a special fencer's sleep mask. Come on," I said. "That movie is all about sleep. Why do you think he writes Z's everywhere?"

Ed's argument was that as the awake person, *I* should have to wear the uncomfortable headwear.

We were inching toward the marriage counselor's couch when in the nick of time, I found a product called Light Wedge: "The only personal reading light that has the ability to save the 50 percent of marriages that end in divorce." It's a thin, glowing slice of acrylic that lies on the page, enabling one to read "in the dark without keeping his or her partner awake with an irksome reflection."

I settled in with my Light Wedge and a bowl of chips. "Happy now?"

"No," said Ed. "You get crumbs in the bed and steal the blankets. I'm still going to want that divorce."

A married couple can best be defined as a unit of people whose sleep habits are carefully engineered to keep each other awake. I offered to stop eating in bed if Ed would agree to wean himself from his need for multiple pillows. I roll over in the middle of the night and find myself suffocating against a towering mound of goose down. We call it Pillow Mountain.

Ed has fallen for the great marketing ploy of the decade: the decorative pillow ploy. It is no longer enough to buy one pillow per head. There must be a decorative pillow behind one's normal head-resting variety, and a spray of bolsters and scatter pillows in front. Each of these must be of a unique size and shape, so as to require the purchase of a specially fitted pillowcase.

Ed corrected me. "It's called a sham."

No argument here. It's a total sham. To outfit the modern bed with its indulgence of pillows and their little pillow outfits costs hundreds of dollars. Beds now contain entire pillow families, six or seven of them, all nestled together against the headboard, as though watching Leno. "That's okay," I tell them, backing out of the room. "I'll go sleep on the couch."

As we were arguing over the pillow issue, Ed got out of bed to open the bedroom door, which I'd closed so as not to hear the odd poppings and clickings of our refrigerator. Our refrigerator is unique among large appliances, in that it appears to suffer from insomnia. Every night around 4 a.m., it begins shifting, fidgeting and cracking its joints. No doubt it wants some warm milk, which, for a refrigerator, is an existential crisis of considerable weight.

Ed claims not to hear these sounds. He says he needs to have the bedroom door open; otherwise it gets so stuffy he can't sleep. I can't tell him to open a window, because then it'll be too cold. There'll be an all-night struggle for blanket superiority, and no one, to quote Zorro, will catch any Z's. We'll end up out in the kitchen at 4:30, playing cards with the refrigerator.

I know a lot of other couples have similar bedtime issues, and I hope this column has been helpful. I hope this column has the ability to save the 50 percent of marriages that end in divorce. Or that, at the very least, it helps put one of you to sleep.

Picture This

I read something scary today. The Hewlett-Packard company is developing a "wearable, always-on" camera. This is a camera, the article said, that promises to "store your life in images." I don't need this, because I have Ed. Ed is not wearable—except for rare occasions such as heavy air turbulence, wherein he will fasten himself to your arm like a large, distraught handbag—but he is doing a bang-up job of storing our lives in images. At last count, we have 124 photo albums. "Yup," he'll say, "I'm a tourist in my own home."

Ed takes the pictures, and my job is to put them in albums. This enables me to secretly throw away all unflattering shots of myself, leaving the three or so per year in which my mouth is shut and my eyes are open, a combination that still eludes me after years of practice. So it worked out pretty well. Until last month.

Last month Ed bought a camera that takes photos in various sizes, including panoramic. The word panoramic, as you know, comes from the Latin *panor,* meaning "impossible to fit into an album." Ed's camera has an irritating habit of throwing itself, unbeknownst to us, into panoramic mode, forcing me to scissor each picture down to size.

Consequently, about six months ago, I quit doing my job. Ed hasn't noticed yet, because Ed—like 99 percent of the population—has never actually opened an album to revisit a set of photos. Our photos function as a sort of archival record, should the authorities one day call into question, say, our presence at the Half Moon Bay pumpkin patch on October 17, 1993. Your Honor, let the record show that at 11:34 a.m., Ed held two pumpkins up to his chest in an amusing, ribald manner.

The photos are piling up rather alarmingly. One day I will be forced to follow the example of the Nepalese postal service, which, I've heard, can get so far behind that it simply throws away whole sacks of undelivered mail. One day someone in the Nepalese postal service is going to show up to work with a wearable, always-on camera, and someone else is going to be in big, big trouble.

Imagine if we all had the Hewlett-Packard system. The article says your wearable camera will be able to capture 5 frames per second. That is 300 photos per minute, 18,000 per hour, 27,000 per annual visit to the Half Moon Bay pumpkin patch. Handy for those times when loved ones are involved in a disputed finish at the Preakness, but really, logically speaking, who wants this?

I'll tell you who. Those people who make you watch slide shows of their vacation trips, trips apparently funded by the U.S. Geological Survey office, in an effort to document every peak, reservoir, and piney ridge in the region. Our friend Larry does this to us, and you just know he's going to be first in line for the wearable, always-on camera. I'm not having any of it. "Larry," I'm going to say. "I would love to come over and see your photos, but the Petersons are showing security camera footage of their lobby tonight. Apparently there's this moment when the doorman adjusts his jacket that is just riveting."

Not that the "wearable" camera is without merit. It would be mounted on the bridge of your glasses so that it's shooting whatever you're looking at. This way, you don't have to dig it out of your bag and push the proper buttons and compose the shot. Because we all know it takes time to forget to turn on the flash and position your finger just so over the lens. And by then, the moment has passed. Whereas, if you have a constantly snapping digital camera built into your glasses, you will never miss one of life's special moments, though regrettably, most of those moments will now consist of friends and strangers heartlessly mocking your eyewear.

And, since the system is digital, I won't have to worry about putting the trillions of snapshots in albums. I can upload them to "data centers," where they will accumulate to the point that they crash the Internet and world chaos—Finally! Something worth documenting!—ensues.

Driving with Ed

There's a TV ad where Celine Dion is driving all night across some desolate portion of what looks to be the American Southwest. She's singing "I drove all ni-i-i-iight" and she's not singing it quietly. The lyrics suggest she's driving all night because she can't wait to see some guy, presumably that guy with the neatly trimmed white beard who's her husband. Also, the ad implies, she's got a cool car she loves to drive. I'm not buying it. A woman wouldn't drive all night. She'd book a flight so she can arrive on her beloved's doorstep looking washed and cheerful, as opposed to showing up with no sleep and no shower and that sour mouth taste caused by gas-station coffee and worn-out spearmint gum. No woman enjoys driving that much. This is the man's deal: to shift gears while driving too fast on an open road. They live for this.

Alas, they are living a fantasy, for there is no more open

road. The open road is a myth perpetrated by the car industry, which routinely goes around closing off highways and city streets in order to shoot ads featuring vast stretches of open road. These days, only people who drive in the wee hours of the morning, such as bread delivery van drivers and Celine Dion, can make use of five-speed overdrive and rack-and-pinion steering.

Reality does not deter the male driver. The male driver will pretend he is on the Bonneville Salt Flats or the northern reaches of the Kancamagus Highway when in fact he's on the I-80 on-ramp.

My husband, Ed, routinely makes plans to drive to L.A. from San Francisco, simply because he loves to drive. In his mind, he's the man in the Saab turbo ad. He pictures himself flying down the Coastal Highway with the top down and the music up, wearing those funny leather gloves with the holes cut out of the back. Somewhere around Milpitas, it dawns on him that a) taking the coast route will add four hours to his drive, b) we don't own a convertible, and c) people are laughing at the gloves.

Now although the male professes to love driving—to the point where he will waste six hours on a drive that can be flown in one—he must always seek and pursue the shortest possible route to an across-town destination. I give you an actual, unretouched in-car exchange between Ed and our friend Dan:

"You know if you take Clipper Street," Dan is saying, "you can shave six minutes off the drive." These minutes go into a special account, where they can be redeemed for chest hair, leather gloves with holes cut out of the back, and other bonus masculinity awards.

"Not this time of day. That preschool lets out, and the whole right lane's blocked." Ed is making this up. A man will say anything to avoid being exposed as The Guy Who Doesn't Know the Fastest Route. This is right up there, humiliation-wise, with being exposed as The Guy Who Asks for Directions. The deepest shame that can befall an American male is for a stranger in a gas station to find out that—*Oh my God*—you don't know your way around a neighborhood you've never been to.

Meanwhile, Dan's wife, Wendy, and I are across town in her car, trying to find our way back from a matinee. Viewed from above, our route resembles the adorable and random wanderings of a toddler's Etch A Sketch drawings. It is not the most direct route to her house or my house or anything at all—save the mental breaking point of our husbands. But we're fine with it. To a group of women, sitting in a car is little different from sitting in someone's home, only with wheels and not enough closet space. We get caught up in the conversation and forget about the petty details of navigation, such as west vs. east and the like. Wendy crests a hill. "Is that the ocean? How'd we get here?"

So we park the car and go for a walk on the beach. Meanwhile, Dan and Ed have pulled over and come to blows, adding an extra four minutes and a side trip to St. Luke's hospital to their drive time.

Sunshine on a Cloudy Day

It was April, and I was heading for Cleveland. Packing for April is tricky—could be cold, could be hot. I needed a weather report. Normally, I don't bother with weather reports, because I employ my own personal scientific weather reporting system. This consists of a) opening the bedroom window, and b) sticking my arm out and waving it around. It's important to wave it around, so as to get a proper air sample and to keep the neighbors wondering.

This is a roundabout way of explaining why I spent my Tuesday evening watching The Weather Channel. I thought— silly me—that this would be a channel showing nothing but weather reports. I tuned in to find a TV show in progress, called "Storm Stories." Today's storm story involved a bus driver in Florida, about to drive over a causeway just as a tornado was headed his way. "By the time Hugo got to the causeway ..." intoned the narrator darkly. I turned to Ed. "Is Hugo the bus driver or the storm?"

"It's not a hurricane," said Ed. "It's a tornado."

"They don't name tornadoes?"

Ed sighed.

Right about then, just as the drama was reaching its peak, the show cut away to a scene inside the Miami Weather Bureau. A guy named Dave was using a diagram with large red *H*'s and giant moving arrows to explain all about "sucking updrafts." We kept waiting for them to broadcast images of the bus being sucked into the updraft and twirled around like a hamburger wrapper, but this was not to be. The Weather Channel does drama like other channels do weather. That is to say, something of an afterthought.

Then, because several minutes had passed without one, they showed a map of the United States, with shifting dryer lint superimposed on it. There's a rule on The Weather Channel: Five minutes is too long to wait for a map of the United States with dryer lint on it. The lint corresponded to some sort of system, or "front," that was incomprehensible to anyone outside of Weather Service employ. After 30 years of watching fronts move in off the ocean or down from Canada or what have you, I've figured out what it means: It means something cold and wet is going to start falling from the sky, and if it's already falling from the sky, it's going to stop. Why can't forecasters just say this?

Next up was "Evening Edition," which featured two hosts sitting at a credenza, stacking and restacking papers. They did not look like Dave, or any other weather bureau meteorologist. They looked like people who wanted to be on TV news, but did something horribly wrong and were being punished.

"In our top story, a heat wave in New York City..." It appeared that "Evening Edition" didn't tell you the weather; it showed you. The screen featured a shot of people eating ice-cream cones on a Manhattan street. I tried to imagine what the stock-market report would be like if the financial channels took this approach: One shot after another of "suits" exchanging BMWs for Toyotas?

I gave up on The Weather Channel and went ahead and packed. I packed for a heat wave in Cleveland, and I packed for a blizzard. I packed boots and flip-flops and tank tops and a parka. I packed so many layers that I could no longer bring anything to read, which was fine, because I'd need those six hours in flight to berate myself for overpacking. Then I began to worry about what the airport security guard would think when he looked in my bag: "You say you're going to Cleveland, ma'am? It's 90° there. What's the parka for?"

"Well, sir, if you watched The Weather Channel, you would know that several historic Midwest blizzards have actually happened during heat waves. You see, when a front, or 'system,' moves in and the dew point is very high, large red *H*'s and arrows begin to appear in the sky..."

I called my friend in Cleveland. "Do me a favor. Go stick your arm out the window."

You Know the Drill

My husband goes to a dentist who has a TV mounted on the wall beside the chair. Ed comes home talking about the new way of preparing smelts that he saw on the Food Network while the dentist scraped tartar off his incisors. Now, thanks to Ed, I associate seafood dishes with plaque removal, and hardly ever request tartar sauce anymore.

I went to my own dentist this week, after a hiatus of some centuries, and was excited to see that Dr. Chee had installed a TV set too. An infomercial was on, all about porcelain veneers and whitening procedures and other wonderful things that your dental insurance doesn't cover. From observing dozens of Before and After shots, I concluded that women are much better at applying makeup after they get veneers.

The hygienist was draping me with a lead bib, in case some of the X-rays dribbled onto my chest. I asked her if we could change the TV channel. She explained that it was not a TV but rather a VCR for showing videos about Dr. Chee's new services.

Like any successful businessman, Dr. Chee is not one to pass up a revenue-generating opportunity. This is a dentist who hands out free sugar cookies in his waiting room. Dr. Chee is never all that happy to see me, because I never let him replace my fillings. If my teeth don't hurt, I'm not messing with them.

"So," said Dr. Chee. "What brings you here? Need a new toothbrush?"

Dr. Chee told me to watch the video monitor while he poked around in my mouth. On the screen was a closeup of some revolting discolored molars. I waited to see how the porcelain veneer folks were going to tackle this mess.

"These are your teeth." Dr. Chee had been holding a tiny closed-circuit TV camera inside my mouth. He panned from one molar to the next, narrating in the grave, somber tones of a newscaster at the aftermath of a major natural disaster. "Pitted, corroded fillings. Cracks and fissures where the amalgam has pulled away . . ."

He could have said, "Look how nicely these fillings are holding up!" and the images—to my dentally ignorant eye—would have fit. In fact, I'd made the rounds of several other dentists in town, hoping to find one who'd say, "Look how nicely these fillings are holding up!" But they didn't, so I went back to Dr. Chee, where at least you get cookies.

Dr. Chee said that I needed to replace fillings in three teeth and get crowns on two others. He said that a crown costs $850. I have heard of crowns costing this kind of money, but these are mostly in the Tower of London. To distract me from the bad news, he panned artfully to a medium closeup of the roof of my mouth, which he described as a "high, steep vault."

"That's where I keep the gold bullion I'll be using to pay for my dental work," I said. Unfortunately, Dr. Chee had his hand in my mouth, as well as the hand of his lovely assistant and a Bissell dual-suction upright rug-cleaning system and another hand and a 93-piece cordless drill set and the Pensacola University Marching Band.

Consequently my witticism came out this way: "Aast aaa aah caaa aga ah ah at ah ah aaa-aa a caa-ah a ent-ull uh."

Over the years, Dr. Chee has developed a remarkable ability to understand the garbled, consonant-deprived utterances of the orally overloaded. "Ha, ha," he replied.

Then I gave him my usual if-it-ain't-broke line. He turned to the hygienist. "Make a note in the chart: Hold off on replacing fillings until patient's teeth rot in mouth."

He sounded displeased. He sounded like he wanted to send me on a short walk off a long pier with a lead bib.

"Okay, maybe one crown. Will I be better at applying makeup after the procedure?"

Dr. Chee smiled. He's a nice guy, and he doesn't deserve patients like me. If I were him, I'd have put my fist in my mouth a long time ago, and not to fix three fillings.

Check This Out

I'm an enthusiastic fan of the new self-check-in kiosks that the airlines have installed. Having gleefully checked myself in on many occasions, I was eager to try self-check-in's retail cousin, self-checkout. The local Home Depot has four such devices, and last weekend my husband and I paid a visit.

From our cart, Ed handed me one of seven identical piping clamps. I whisked the UPC code over the scanner as I've seen the pros do. Nothing. Ed fished a different clamp from the cart and ran it over the scanner successfully, establishing a baseline of resentment and rancor for our self-checkout experience.

Since the machine seemed to respond to this particular clamp, Ed suggested passing it over the scanner seven times rather than struggling to make the scanner register the UPCs of the other six. The machine took issue with Ed's sensible and innovative checkout strategy.

"Please Place Item in Bagging Area."

"Why?" replied Ed, and here was the start of his undoing. A talking machine will talk to you—endlessly, bossily, repetitively—but it will not, no matter how fascinating or urgent your words, listen to you. It is my belief that these machines infuriate men because they remind them of the less pleasing aspects of talking to their spouses.

"Please Place Item in Bagging Area."

I put a bag onto the bag holder, and Ed dropped the six clamps into it. Now the machine had a new gripe. *"Unexpected Item in Bagging Area. Please Remove Item."*

As it turned out, there was a scale underneath the bagging area, enabling the machine to ensure that the two-ounce clamp you scanned is exactly what goes into the bag, rather than the two-ounce clamp plus the Makita cordless drill kit you are endeavoring to steal.

From the cart, Ed next picked up an eight-foot length of conduit pipe. The UPC code sticker had been placed midway along the shaft. Scanning the thing would entail knocking over a display caddy of roofing tiles and Roof Wear Warning Signals ("1. Loose granules . . .") located on the far side of the machine, while simultaneously tripping up customers passing by behind us.

At a store that sells lumber and toilets and bags of cement, self-checkout isn't a convenience—it's a Chevy Chase movie.

Ed was perturbed, and this takes some doing. Ed is the most level-headed person I know. You could take one of the carpenter's levels from Aisle 5 and place it on his head and the little bubble will always be right there in the middle. I mention this by way of explaining why it was that at this particularly tense juncture, I chose to further aggravate my husband by idly asking what's inside the little bubble on a carpenter's level.

Ed looked as if he was trying to decide who—me or the machine—more clearly deserved to have their granules whacked loose with a conduit pipe.

"Liquid," he said, in a not overwhelmingly cordial tone.

In any other store, I might have stalked off to go flirt with the customers. This isn't possible at Home Depot. A man in Home Depot can't even *see* a woman.

A woman appeared at our side with a handheld scan gun and a marriage counselor. She explained that self-checkout was for small items only, and then she scanned the piping and reset the machine. Though self-checkout has enabled Home Depot to hire fewer checkout clerks, it has had to hire instead a team of special self-checkout troubleshooters.

I asked the woman how her new job was going. She looked like she was ready for self-checkout of the personal, I-quit variety. "Sometimes customers get so mad they throw stuff on the floor and walk away." And then the self-checkout machine makes them sleep on the couch.

The Naked Truth

Once you hit 40, it is time to think twice about miniskirts. Also, string bikinis, midriff-baring tops, skintight or low-rise jeans that have been sanded white the length of the thighs, as though the wearer had been tied to a bumper and dragged facedown around the block a few times. These are clothes for young people.

Alas, this is what the stores are selling. Today's popular clothing chains appeal strictly to teenagers, who can be counted upon to change their tastes every 30 days, as the latest *Cosmo Girl* or *Teen Vogue* arrives in the mail. Customers like me cannot possibly afford new clothing more than once a decade, owing to the financial strain of paying for teenage children's rapidly shifting fashion needs. So no one bothers to make clothing for us.

This is a dangerous situation. Expose a middle-aged woman to nothing but miniskirts and abbreviated tops for long enough, and she's bound to cave. One day, when her self-esteem is dangerously high and the dressing room lights dangerously low, she'll try on something designed for her daughter and say to herself, "Oh, why not?" If she happens to be shopping with her children, the answer to this question will be provided for her. But middle-aged husbands offer no such reality check. They live in a candy-land of denial and residual carnality. They still, bless them, like to see a little flesh.

My husband recently made me try on a bikini. A bikini is not so much a garment as a cloth-based reminder that your parts have been migrating all these years. My waist, I realized that day in the dressing room, has completely disappeared beneath my rib cage, which now rests directly on my hips. I'm exhibiting continental drift in reverse.

The buttocks, too, have overrun their boundaries, infringing on territory that rightly belongs to the thighs. I have encouraged my thighs to do something about this—restraining order, guard dog—but they have not. Your thighs are rarely there for you.

"Cute!" says Ed dementedly. "Turn around."

"You turn around first."

Ed does not understand what all women my age understand. The mature lady's buttock does not wish to come out and take a bow. Designers of mature ladies' swimwear know this. They've built little curtains into their designs, enabling the sagging buttock to keep hidden, and/or cast votes in privacy. God help me, I've entered the Age of Skirted Swimwear. This is the age right after Accessorizing with Reading Glasses and a few years before Can't Name Anyone on the Radio.

Even the knees are in on the betrayal. I recently saw a tabloid photograph of a 40-something Demi Moore with her knees circled in red, highlighting the fact that they were disappearing under the shifting shoals of her thighs. *Ha-ha,* I said to myself. Just deserts for having a face and breasts (and a boyfriend) that look 25. Then I looked at my own knees, which I plan never to do again.

The foot is more or less the one body part that time leaves alone. Well into your 70s, you can wear whatever style shoes you feel like wearing. Positioned, as they are, at the bottom of the heap, gravity is not an issue. Or so I thought. Shortly after the swimsuit debacle, I tried on a pair of pointy-toed black pumps, the sort that actresses on *Sex and the City* were wearing for 30 days back in spring.

"How do those work for you?" the salesgirl asked. I told her they were pinching me, and not in an appreciative, you-look-just-like-that-gal-on-*Sex and the City* way.

"You know," she said brightly, "your feet flatten as you age."

I went to find Ed, and I told him about my flattening instep. He smiled and put his arm around me. That still fits, and for this I'm happy.

Bug Off!

As far as my husband, Ed, is concerned, the greatest thing about the Great Outdoors is that it remains outdoors. In particular, Ed hates ants.

"I don't hate ants," Ed will insist. "I just want them to live in their own houses. I don't go barging into their homes un-invited, do I?" Ed would have you believe that it's a matter of etiquette, of shoddy ant manners, and that if we'd gotten to know the ants, come to think of them as our friends, he'd be happy to have them over. *Six thirty, then? Great! Will the soldiers be coming or just the workers?*

I tell him to ignore them, because they'll be gone when the rain ends and their homes stop flooding. I care about drowning ants because once I left my cousin's Ant Farm outside when it rained, and the farmers all died. I guess I'm still working through the guilt. Whatever the reason, I think of our kitchen as a port in the storm, an ant refugee camp, providing crumbs and shelter in time of need.

Ed just wants to slay them. And there are products on the market to help him do this. They tend to come in two categories. The first appeals to the man who loves a good battle, especially one where the enemy is unarmed and the size of Wheatena. These products have names like Maxforce and the aggressive if ungrammatical Real Kill.

Ed knows better than to try to get UN approval for this sort of thing. He knows I believe in a humane, organic approach. I once got Ed to stop killing the spiders in our bedroom by telling him the spiders eat the ants. Of course, this isn't true. Unlike humans, spiders are no good at what my mother used to call "drawing ants." They do not leave wet Popsicle sticks on windowsills or open honey jars out on counters. Ed bought my theory, but only for a while. I'd come into the room and see him on his hands and knees in the corner, inspecting the webs. "If I don't see ants by Friday, you're in trouble, my friend."

Pesticide companies understand the husband-wife ant dynamic. Many have a separate line that emphasizes the nontoxic quality of the products, which is quite a bold marketing move for what is essentially a weapon of mass destruction.

One company tries to make ant death seem like a holiday in France. They have a product called Ant Café, so that rather than picturing the little guys gasping and writhing, you picture them sipping bowls of café au lait, smoking Gitanes and leafing through *Le Figaro,* which is hard to do at the same time unless, like the ant, you have six hands.

The last spray bottle Ed brought home was a brand

called Safer's. He read to me from the label, pausing now and again to make ant pâté on the counter. "It combines bait with borax," he said, as though this made any kind of sense, as though helping them have whiter whites had always been the idea. "Fresh Mint Odor, honey!"

I've never encountered this kind of fresh mint odor. Imagine smelling some mint that's growing on the lawn of a petrochemical plant. It's *that* kind of fresh mint odor. When Ed wasn't looking, the Safer's went away on a holiday in France.

For a long time, Ed didn't say much about the ants and I thought he'd made his peace with them. Then I found some of those little ant cups that leak brown, sticky, evil stuff and do not match our décor. He thought I'd like this idea, because no spraying and dying-on-the-countertops was involved. "They take the poison home and die there!" Ed said cheerfully.

I did not like the idea and I said so. So we had a little argument about the ant cups. Things may have gotten a tiny bit out of hand. I may have threatened to get some "jerk cups" and put them out in the places Ed goes to feed. A door slammed at some point. The ants watched for a while, and then fled for their lives. We haven't seen them since.

Mr. Fix-It-Later

Kitchen renovation is a virus that preys upon the middle-aged homeowner. We caught it from our friends Dave and Kate, who caught it from Bill and Adair, who got it from reading magazines like *Martha Stewart Living*. We didn't have the requisite $20,000 on hand, so Ed announced he'd build the cabinets himself. I recall the moment clearly, the way people recall where they were when JFK was shot or the Mets won the '69 World Series.

Let me give you some perspective here. Our bathroom faucet is enameled with faux porcelain that has begun to chip off. Early in 1996, Ed purchased a tube of something called Porc-a-Fix, intending to fill in the chips. I came across the Porc-a-Fix, unopened and in its original packaging, inside a kitchen drawer recently. So long had it been that I no longer recalled the original purpose of the product and took it to be some sort of ham seasoning.

Ed looked at the tube. "I'll get to that this weekend," he said. Home repair projects around our house generally fall into two categories: "I'll get to that this weekend" and "I'll get to that this summer." Followed by an eventual shift to a third category: "I'll get the Yellow Pages."

Make no mistake, my husband is a highly competent man. He has laid hardwood floors, put up walls, installed skylights. Most of this he did during a period of unemployment in his 20s. These days he works a full-time job, and thus spends his time off avoiding anything that sounds like work. If woodworking were called, say, "relaxing with wood," things might actually get built.

The other problem is that guy Norm Abram. Abram hosts the PBS show *Yankee Workshop,* which is misleading, because you picture Nathan Hale stooped in some low-ceilinged, poorly lit Connecticut basement. When in reality, Norm Abram's workshop is the size of the Vatican. Norm has every power tool ever invented. His workshop is airy and bright and well heated.

"Now I'm just going to walk over here and switch on my laminate trimmer," Norm will say, and men across America go, "Yes! I'm going to go switch on my laminate trimmer too!" And then they get to the basement and their wives have laundry on the workbench, and mice are living in the biscuit joiner, and it's cold and dank, and upstairs the Cubs are playing the Marlins, and that is pretty much that. In the case of the kitchen cabinet project, it's not Norm's fault. It's Charlie's. Charlie is a friend of Ed's, who recently—in the time it would take Ed to unearth the cordless drill and go find batteries for it, make a sandwich, see if the Cubs are still ahead and nod off on the sofa—redid his kitchen.

I pointed out that Charlie is retired.

"Good idea," said Ed. He was all set to retire too. "With all the money we'll be saving by making our own furniture, why..."

I reminded Ed about the marble-top sideboard incident. Some years back, Ed found a piece of marble at a bargain price somewhere and decided to build a dining room sideboard around it. This required the purchase of a lathe and the aforementioned biscuit joiner, plus all the wood: an outlay of some $500. If he'd actually made the thing, we might still have come out ahead. Instead we came out with a slab of marble and some costly rodent housing.

I try to get Ed to focus on smaller projects—for instance, picture framing. Three years ago he took me up on this and bought a miter box and a mount cutter. For three years now, photographs and artwork have been piling up in the den. Every now and then, you hear them talking to one another as you pass by.

"How long you been waiting here?"

"'Bout a year. But I hear he's got the miter box and everything. Just the other day I heard him say he's going to get to it this weekend."

The Beer and Bacon Diet

The chickens were the first to go. Ed—Ed's my husband—had read something about the hormones they're injected with. "They're growing breasts!" he said with great alarm. I could not see the problem here.

"They're chickens, honey," I said. "That's their job."

Ed was envisioning some sort of biotech nightmare: vamping hens in training bras and eye shadow. From now on, he decreed, we were to buy only free-range organic chickens. Ed would put them in the shopping cart. I'd look at the price and take them out. "Are we eating them or putting them through college?" I said.

Beef went next. Because I used to write for a health magazine, I had heard about Mad Cow disease back when it was known by its scientific nomenclature, bovine spongebob empopalopathy. I got the entire family worked into a frenzy. I'd hold up a slice of Swiss cheese and say, "Your brain looks just like this!" I might have overdone it. One day when Ed brought his daughter Phoebe to the office, a co-worker asked, "How are you, Phoebe?" Phoebe was eight at the time. "I have Mad Cow disease," she said.

To avoid Mad Cow, I'm told, you should eat only organic grass-fed beef. These cows are not raised in pens or fed commercial feed. They go to the same college as the free-range chickens.

So that left fish, but not for long. Sometime last year, there was a story in the news about mercury levels in ocean-caught fish. They made it sound like you could pick up a tuna and put its tail under your tongue and a little silver bar would shoot up the side and tell you if you had a fever. (Of course you can't do this, because a tuna tail is too big to fit under your tongue.) I started buying fish-farm fish, but Ed hadn't recovered from his chickens-with-bosoms fright. "You don't know what they're feeding them," he said.

He turned out to be right. Six months later came a report about PCBs in farm-raised salmon. Apparently they feed them fish meal made from ground-up fish that feed in polluted parts of the Atlantic. "They feed fish fish!" I said and immediately regretted it. Soon we'd be reading about piscine spongebob empopalopathy.

I was about to reprise my Swiss cheese demonstration, but then I realized I'd thrown the cheese away because it contains dairy fats. These are saturated fats that raise your bad cholesterol level. Bad cholesterol is the kind that clogs arteries, shoplifts lipsticks and lies under oath.

So Ed and I were eating a lot of vegetables. Vegetables on pasta, vegetables on rice. This was extremely healthy, until you got to the part where Ed and I are found in the kitchen at 10 p.m., feeding on Froot Loops and tubes of cookie dough.

Next the Atkins diet hit, and carbohydrates became evil and fattening. So we had to abandon the rice and pasta too. It finally happened: Everything we could afford to eat was bad for us. For dinner last week, we ate steamed vegetables and a tiny piece of Alaskan river salmon. These fish come from pristine waters where prospectors once panned for gold, until salmon became more valuable. The hunger set in while I was loading the dishwasher. We had no snack foods or breakfast cereals to appease our hunger, because they contain transfats and high-fructose corn syrup, which cause your arteries to race around the block and tie themselves in knots.

Ed rummaged through the freezer. He found some bacon in the back. It had been so long since we'd had bacon that we couldn't recall what was bad about it, so we fried it up fast before we remembered.

Then Ed took out two beers. I told him I'd read something about breast cancer levels and alcohol.

He said he wasn't a chicken, twisted off the cap, and raised the bottle. "To your health!"

Menu Madness

You always know when a waiter is about to recite the specials. It's like that awkward moment in a musical when the lead guy is about to break into song again. Everyone around him tries to be polite, but inside they're going, "NOOO!!! Be a normal person!" NOOO! Just write it on a chalkboard!

Last week I went to a restaurant where they don't recite specials. They actually write it all down. Unfortunately, they write it in a mixture of Italian and food-ese, necessitating a half-hour vocabulary lesson. I don't do well in these places. I'm happiest in a restaurant that calls its sauces Louis, or "red." I don't want to know which organic farm the produce grew up on, and I don't want to hear the adjective *heirloom* unless I'm watching *Antiques Roadshow. Do you know what you've got here? It's a tomato. It's worth about $45. . . .*

I was out at a new Italian place with some girlfriends last week. We were thinking of ordering an antipasto platter, which included "House-made *salumi.*"

"You've got a typo here," said Adair to the waiter.
He replied that, no, *salumi* meant "cured meat." "*Salumi*
is the generic category. Salami is *salumi,* but *salumi* is not
salami." Soon someone would be breaking into song about
how they say "tomato," and I'd have to leave.

Kathy ordered first. She was considering the "*Bigoli
all'amatriciana* with house-cured *guanciale.*" She happened
to know that *guanciale* was pork cheek, and for some reason felt this was a plus. She asked the waiter what *Bigoli*
was. He said *Bigoli* was the name of the pasta machine.

So we consulted amongst ourselves. We didn't want to
be rude. "And . . . what comes out of the machine tonight?"

"It's an extruded pasta." It was spaghetti. Spaghetti
with red sauce. Talk about cheek.

Adair ordered next. She had some questions about the
rabbit. The menu described it as "Rosemary-braised rabbit
with rabbit offal *spiedino.*"

"What is offal *spiedino*?" said Adair, accenting the second syllable of each word, so as to suggest she spoke Italian. The waiter said that *spiedino* meant "on skewers."

"Yes, but what's on the skewers? What is *oh-fall*?"

"Heart, kidneys and liver wrapped in *pancetta* and . . ."
Offal was offal.

The lesson being taught here is that it is better not to
ask. If you ask, then you run the risk of knowing. For instance, we now also know that hanger steak is cut from
"the muscle that pushes the food from one stomach to the
other."

My other beef—sorry, complaint—with menu language is that the hyphen is underused, often with alarming consequences. For instance, in the phrase "Grilled Potter Family Farm beef heart," what is grilled? The Potter family? Their farm? Whose heart is it? The cow's or Mr. Potter's?

I have seen with my own two eyes a menu offering "Mesquite grilled alligator pepper crusted pork tenderloin." Fortunately, by the time I got to the end of the phrase, I'd forgotten the beginning of it, so it was just some pork thing.

Because of the excess verbiage on menus these days, the desserts have run over onto their own separate pieces of paper. This gives them plenty of room to stretch out and make no sense.

Kathy noticed a red-wine risotto, which had apparently escaped from the entrées page—or was it the wine list?—and was masquerading as a sweet.

We went straight to the check. I put my hand on the tray and used the muscle that pushes the bill from one diner to another.

"Your treat this time, right?" I said to Adair.

"Cacciucco!" said Adair, which is either an Italian curse word or an entrail, I forget.

Is That What You're Wearing?

Every Saturday evening in households across America, a predictable scene unfolds. A couple is dressing for dinner out. One of them looks great. In our house, this would be Ed. Unlike myself, Ed can always find a top and a bottom that complement each other, or at the very least refrain from throwing things at each other.

Meanwhile, I am lolling on the couch, nursing the delusion that the jeans with the grease stains on one thigh and the Polarfleece pullover that appears to be stealing the dog's fur one hair at a time, and making admirable progress, will be just fine.

Inevitably, the couple must come together and the words must be spoken: "You're wearing that?"

"What?" I'll say. This is a stalling tactic, allowing me time to pull together a defense of denim as appropriate dinner-party attire. I point out that I'll be seated at a table, and thus no one will see me from the waist down.

Unfortunately, this leads us to the waist-up portion of the argument. As there is no logical argument for wearing a garment that features armpit zippers to a dinner party, I am forced down the path of illogical argument: "Einstein wore sneakers to the Nobel Prize dinner." Actually, this isn't so much illogical as untrue. Ed ignores me and goes back to his cuff links, whatever those are.

I consider accessorizing my outfit, but this is a skill that eludes me. I tie neckwear the way Brownies do—or Pony Express riders. The last time I wore a scarf, Ed put his hands in the air. "Don't shoot," he said.

I stopped bothering with jewelry ages ago. Sometimes I open my jewelry box and look inside with a sort of archaeologist's fascination. How queer this strand of red stones. What was its purpose?

It's been so long since I wore earrings that the holes in my lobes have completely closed up. I told this to a friend recently, and she claims a similar thing happened to her waist. After about ten years of wearing nonfitted stretch waistbands, she insists that her waistline has completely disappeared.

I don't know what happened to me. I used to derive great joy from dressing up. These days joy takes the form of getting away with wearing the same thing two days in a row. My idea of dressing up has become not wearing lug soles. I suppose I'm not being fair to Ed. I should dress up for him, if only so that other husbands don't feel sorry for him. Poor Ed. Look what he married. It's a cocker spaniel, isn't it?

Some people would argue that dressing nicely becomes more important as you age. If you think of your face as a piece of clothing that you are forced to wear, day in and day out, and that eventually this very key wardrobe piece becomes wrinkled and spotted and ill-fitting, the least you can do is pair it with something that looks smart and crisp. This way, the total look averages out better. I can see these people's point. I can see it, and yet I don't care.

Part of the reason I don't care is that most of the people around me don't seem to care either. It's as though somewhere along the line, without saying or signing anything, America reached an agreement: If we all pull together and look like hell, we can make this country great. We can be people who don't feel the edges of our waistbands! We can be people wearing sweat suits in the airports of Europe! One nation, undivided, with Velcro and stretch panels for all.

Good House Hunting

Our poor realtor. She's sent us listings for 16 weeks, and we haven't found a place we want. The other day—true story—we saw a listing that said "yard, complete with outhouse." Another included the phrase "classic midcentury tunnel entrance."

Had the century in question been the 15th, and had the home come with a moat and the threat of enemy attack, I could see where the tunnel might be a selling point. But this was a 1952 house.

One listing bragged of "solid surface" countertops. Fabulous, I thought, because our last house had liquid countertops, and we had to hire skin divers to get to the spice rack.

We're like that finicky Persian cat in the old Friskies ads that turned its nose up at everything its owner fed it. (It's difficult to turn up a nose that is already so far turned up as to have penetrated the sinus cavities, but this cat managed it.)

Still, it's been a learning experience. For instance, we have learned the origins of the term In-Law Apartment. This is a basement living area so low ceilinged and devoid of light you would never move your own parents in, but your wife's parents would fit right in, alongside any enemy soldiers you've hauled from the moat and shackled to the walls.

Once we've whittled down the choices, the fun begins. For all of you who make a habit of looking in friends' medicine cabinets when you're over for dinner, the Open Home tour is not to be missed. Though the ensuing gossip is less titillating, as you don't know whom it's about. Psst, some people on 44th Street in Oakland use beard mascara.

Unfortunately, these days, most Open Homes have been cleared of the owner's belongings and "staged" with generically tasteful Pottery Barn furniture and accessories. It's as though there are whole neighborhoods populated by people who own nothing but brocade throw pillows and eat only colorful Italian dry goods, positioned with their labels facing forward. Often, the staging includes a breakfast tray of croissants and coffee lying on the bed, as though the homeowners had been abruptly chased out and left to wander the streets in their pajamas. Frequently, they've left so quickly that the fire is still burning. Ed will kneel down and inspect the fireplace. "We just missed them, Kemo Sabe," he'll say.

Last week, I caught Ed eating the staging. On a table out on the deck, a plate of strawberries had been placed alongside a chilled bottle of wine and two glasses. Ed believed they were treats set out to win us over, like the chocolate-chip cookies Realtors will bake just prior to your visit in an attempt to mask evil odors seeping up from the in-law quarters.

This afternoon, Ed has been threatening to visit the upstairs bathroom for reasons other than having a look. Ed's GI tract is timed to go off about three hours after the second cup of Sunday morning coffee, i.e., during our afternoon house hunt. This means he routinely faces the existential torment of an endless array of pristine toilets, all of them off-limits.

Ed looks at our map. "Which place had the outhouse?"

Perhaps this is our problem. Perhaps we're paying too much attention to the cookies and the pillows and the old people moaning in the cellar, and not enough to the actual house. However, I remain confident that one day, when neither of us is expecting it, we will walk into a house, look at each other and say, "This is it." And our Realtor, like the exasperated Persian cat owner, will sigh with relief and collapse onto a tasteful arrangement of brocade pillows.

Counter Attack

It is my personal belief that the people who install the mirrors and lighting in department store dressing rooms are in direct cahoots with the cosmetic companies. All down the rows of rooms, you hear the sad moans and horrified gasps of women confronted with their own fluorescent-lit reflections. My eye bags, I realized the other day while shopping with my friend Wendy, had ceased to be an anatomical feature and were approaching the status of an actual piece of luggage. "You can almost see the little handles," I wailed. Wendy was in the next room trying on a jacket. "My skin is green," she was saying. I assured Wendy it was light reflecting off the jacket. "But the jacket is brown," she said.

We went directly from there to the makeup department, where a facialist determined that we needed help; a whole new approach. As with all major renovations, this one was to begin with foundation. I told the salesgirl I don't like foundation, because it sinks into my wrinkles and makes them look even deeper, if you can imagine any deeper wrinkles than the kind I've got. She could not, of course, for she was 19 and the only wrinkles she owned were the kind that appear on her nose when forced to contemplate the horrors of middle-aged skin.

"That's because you're not using a primer," said the girl. Her name was Elaine. Her company actually sells a product called Face Primer. "You wouldn't paint a room without putting on primer first, would you?"

"Of course not," I said, because my husband was not around to expose me as a liar. We recently painted our den and I had tried to argue for a single coat. Why spend an extra two days painting when you could just put a lower wattage bulb in the overhead light?

In keeping with the home repair theme, this brand of makeup was to be put on with brushes. The salesgirl, who had gotten me into the makeover chair, was applying primer with one such brush. She suggested buying their four-pack of specialized makeup brushes, which came in a pink leatherette case. "It's an investment," she said. Did that mean that over time the brushes would become more valuable, and that one day I could cash them in and retire? It did not. It meant they were very expensive. The foundation brush alone cost $42.

"What is it, mink?" I asked. I was trying to be funny, but the line landed far shy of its mark, for the brush was, in fact, Siberian blue squirrel. "I've never seen a blue squirrel," Wendy commented.

"Now you know why," I said. I pictured entry-level

makeup company flacks, sent out to stalk the northern forests with BB guns.

"Maybe they just trim their little tails and let them go," Wendy said charitably.

Elaine said that my brush portfolio would last 10 to 15 years if I took care of the bristles. This entailed using the company's Brush Bath and Brush Cleanser. "You want to treat them like your own hair," Elaine said. She was wrong. I wanted to treat them like squirrels treat their own hair. Shouldn't that be enough?

Elaine wasn't listening. She had moved on. She was applying a $35 skin luminizer, which, she said, "minimizes fine lines." For instance, the fine line between luminous skin and highway robbery.

"That is so pretty on you," said Elaine. Notice the structure of this sentence. It is the makeup that's pretty, not me. Wendy told me I had a bad attitude, that I looked fabulous. She handed me a mirror. I had to admit that I looked, if not fabulous, a bit less washed out.

I considered buying it all: foundation, makeup, makeup remover, primer, sealant, luminizer, cleanser, moisturizer, brushes, brush cleanser, brush bath, brush masseuse, brush finishing school ... Instead, I went down the street to the hardware store and bought some 25-watt bulbs.

Unpopular Mechanics

My old mechanic, Stephen Lee, was an honest man. One morning I had my car towed to his garage with a note affixed, stating, "Will not start!!"

He called my office to tell me that the reason it wouldn't start was that the gas tank was empty. He could have lied and said it was the starter. Then he said, "I'm charging you $50—because you're stupid!" which was possibly more honesty than was called for, but so be it.

Stephen Lee retired early, an event I take no small amount of credit for, having owned a sickly 1966 Volvo these past ten years. I did not take the news well, for it meant finding another mechanic. I do not trust car mechanics. I don't know anything about engines, because I, like other women, lack the take-apart gene.

From a young age, the male feels a powerful need to pry the backs off mechanical objects and disassemble them to see what makes them tick. If the family is lucky, the compulsion will strike just before the picture tube or what-have-you would have blown or otherwise stopped ticking on its own.

The female does not share this compulsion, except when it comes to men she is dating. Many's the time I've tried to open up Ed and see what makes him tick (neurosis and bran, so far as I've been able to figure out).

Anyway, men understand motors and women don't. You may say that this is a stereotype, and I won't argue with you because I know even less about stereos than I know about cars. So your male mechanic can say to your female car owner, "You've got a fraying bammy crank in your left vorculator, and your frunchions are shot. Gonna run you $700," and there's no way for us to know if this is true or if, in fact, it's his home entertainment center that needs the new vorculator.

My new mechanic, Andy, seems like a nice enough fellow. I base this primarily on the fact that he breeds parakeets in a little aviary inside the shop. Though part of me believes there's a how-to book out there for shady car mechanics that includes the line: "Set up a parakeet aviary. Women will think you're nice."

I recently took my car in for a tune-up, hoping this would solve the problem it was having. "When I hit the gas, it goes, 'UNH UNH UNH UNH UNH,'" I said intelligently. Andy took notes while I talked, and nodded, like a concerned therapist, though for all I know the notes said, "Total ding-dong. Give her the fraying bammy crank story."

Andy's theory was that water and "sediment" had been

getting into the gas tank through my ill-fitting gas cap. This would cost $450 because, being men, they had to take apart the whole rear end of the car to get the tank out and clean it up.

"Can't you just clean it out with a suction thingie?"

There was a pause, while Andy debated whether it was worth $450 to hang up and never have to listen to my voice again. "I don't have a 'suction thingie.'"

Andy said I was putting the cart before the horse. I'm not sure what he meant by this, but a horse and cart sounded pretty appealing right about then.

Then he said, "If I do it your way, will you sign a form saying 'Mary Roach agrees that this might not work and that she won't yell at me if it doesn't?'" I considered the possibility that Andy was an honest man and that my car was the more appropriate target for my anger. I agreed to do it his way and spent the $450. As usual, I went away feeling like a sucker. Or a suction thingie. But let's not get technical.

Congested and Confused

When I was young, a nose had few choices when it came to cold remedies. There were the capsules filled with cupcake sprinkles, and there was the antifreeze-looking stuff with its own little medicine cup. There was also that nasal spray bottle that breathed in and out in the TV ads, but frankly, this was unnerving. It was like having a tiny obscene phone caller living in your medicine cabinet.

It's not so simple anymore. Today's cold sufferer must confront The Wall of Cold Remedies. There are pills for people with stuffy noses and pills for people with nasal congestion, who are, I suspect, simply people with stuffy noses and advanced degrees, or, otherwise put, stuffy people with stuffy noses. Perhaps because I don't have an advanced degree, I don't understand some things. For example, the difference between sinus congestion and nasal congestion. Fortunately, there are helpful anatomical drawings on the boxes. These tell us that the sinuses are the sink drain located over the upper nose, whereas the nasal passages are the dripping faucet down below.

Possibly a cheaper and faster remedy would be to have Ed, my husband, use a plunger on me. The facial suction marks would be a source of embarrassment, but no worse than the embarrassment endured by the guy on the 24-Hour box with the clock installed on his head. Every day at noon he has to pry the hour hand out of his eye socket. No doubt there's a special pill for that too.

I'm not a fan of what the drug companies call "cocktail" remedies: a single pill that treats nasal congestion, cough, headache, fever, sore throat, loose shingles, rising interest rates, pushy salesmen, cracked O-rings, and a dozen other things you don't actually have. Especially puzzling is the combination of a cough suppressant and expectorant. Why would you seek to "loosen chest congestion," readying it for travel, and at the same time shut down the launching mechanism?

Seeking the gentle simplicity of yesteryear, I reached for the bottle of NyQuil with its adorable medicine cup hat. Then I stopped. There's a DayQuil now too. Soon there would be a Dusk-quil, and a Daylight-Savings-quil, and a Darkest-Hour-Just-Before-the-Dawn-quil. Then my gaze strayed two shelves down, to something entirely new and possibly fabulous: Breathe Right vapor nasal strips. These are a variation of the nose strips you see football players wearing. Instead of simply trying to unclog the mess inside your nostrils, the Breathe Right strip holds them open wider, so there's room for everything: congestion, airflow, toilet plunger, movie tickets. Plus, you enjoy the unique motivational pick-me-up of feeling like a linebacker. Rather than lying around the house moaning for soup, you find yourself up and about, grunting and shoving. People laugh at your shiny nylon trousers and you hurl them to the ground! You dislocate their bones, and when you're done, an NFL pension awaits. Way to feel better!

There is one more thing to keep in mind (that's the area above and to the rear of the sink drain). If you take a pill that cures all your cold symptoms, no one will know you are sick. No one will pity you or let you out of your chores or tell you to take the rest of the afternoon off and read junky magazines in bed. There should be a pill that, while easing your overall distress, leaves intact one or two of the showier symptoms, the sympathy-getters. Whoever comes up with this pill will become very rich, so rich he can afford his own mansion, and another for his mother, and one for the heavy breather in his medicine cabinet.

I Married a Pack Rat

For the past decade, my husband's excuse for not going through his old LPs was that he'd do it when we move. We're moving on Saturday. The replacement excuse is that he doesn't have time because he has too much packing to do. One could make the point that there'd be less packing to do if he'd toss some of his stuff. Bracing for high seas, one does.

"So you're calling this junk?" Ed is holding aloft a Tony Bennett album.

I am skating on thin ice here. Possibly I'm already down in the pond water, thrashing about with my skates. "Not specifically."

Ed says that many of his LPs are irreplaceable. I recognize this argument. I believe I used it in explaining why I did not throw away, among other priceless items, a Pan Am airsickness bag, some rocks from the Arctic Circle with pretty orange lichen on them, and a 1987 USDA press release entitled "Milestones in Dairy History." But in those instances, it was my argument, and so it made excellent sense.

I press on. "But if you never listen to any of these albums, why would you want to replace them?"

Attempting to apply common sense in these scenarios is useless. I know this. Earlier in the week, I tried to discard a box of expired Super-8 movie film for which Ed has no camera. He vetoed the move, stating that he might one day find a Super-8 camera in a Goodwill store. Also vetoed was the throwing away of two shelves of college paperbacks. The pages were yellowed, and there was mildew on the covers. If you listened carefully you could hear them reaching out and making friends with my lichen. "Some of these books have meaning to me," said Ed, and then he paused. "I just don't know what the meaning is."

I recently read an article about hoarding in the animal kingdom. The male black wheatear bird, the article said, collects piles of heavy stones before the mating season. "Those with the largest piles are more likely to mate," the story explained and at the same time didn't really explain. If I should die suddenly—which seems more and more likely as the week wears on—Ed should consider expanding his dating pool to include female wheatear birds. I'll make a note of it in my will.

Ed tries to explain why he would want to keep a pile of records he never listens to. "It's just knowing that they're there. That I could listen to them if I wanted to." I remind him that his turntable doesn't work. "So, actually you can't listen to them." Which reminds me. I pick up the turntable and put it on the designated throwaway pile, which I had envisioned at the beginning of this undertaking as a towering, teetering mound engulfing most of our front entryway and portions of the sidewalk, but is in reality closer in size to the little mounds of toenail parings Ed occasionally stacks up on the bedside table. These are, happily, replaceable, and I encounter only token resistance when I throw them away.

"You can't throw the turntable out. It belongs to Andrea." Andrea is his ex-wife.

"So let's return it to her."

Ed looks genuinely puzzled. "It's broken. Why would she want it?"

In the end, we compromised. He kept some, and he sold some. He forgave me for the anguish I'd caused him, because he was able to get $240 for his LPs at the new and used music store. This he used to buy 31 used CDs, which take up not quite but almost the same square footage as the LPs, and will impress the heck out of the next female wheatear who comes to town.

Makes Scents

We just moved into a new house, and it has smell ghosts: pockets of mystery odors that the previous owner left behind, along with wiper fluid and a bag of frankfurters which, like cats, are busily marking their territory in the refrigerator. Soon our own odors will set up camp and conquer the smell world of the previous owner, but in the meantime, I thought we could use some professional help.

"People today are more actively involved in their 'smell' world." These are the words of a "scent expert" from Brown University. The expert's words are being used to help promote an electronic gizmo that plays the latest CDs—not music, or books on tape. Just odors. It's the new Scentstories fragrance disc player, whose inventors seem not very actively involved in their capitalization and spacing world.

The marketing material said that the twenty-five Scentstories on the five discs were chosen by a leading fragrance-design firm, from "a pool of more than 1,000 creative scent possibilities." Here was a pool I plan to stay out of, at least without my wet suit.

The idea behind a "multiple scent experience"—instead of a solitary scent experience, as most room fresheners and perfumes and aging hot dogs provide—is that this way the nose can't adapt to the scent and stop smelling it. The discs advance to a new scent every half hour, to keep the nose on its toes.

As with CDs, both the scent discs and the individual scent selections have names—in this case, names like "Following the Winding Creek," and "Shades of Vanilla." Unlike CDs, there is no performer, though I suspect Yanni might somehow be involved. I chose the disc entitled "Wandering Barefoot on the Shore." The scents were pleasant, but I did not recognize them as ocean- or foot-related. Barring oil spills or salt or dying marine life, I would be hard-pressed to describe a shore scent.

I switched discs and fast-forwarded to the second cut: "Picking Peachy Freesias." I asked Ed to tell me what the air smelled like. He answered that it smelled like the bathrooms at the car wash after they've been cleaned.

Interestingly, Ed considered this a positive comment. Ed enjoys the scent story of the car wash bathrooms. I can't say for sure, but I feel it is unlikely Ed will one day be employed by a leading fragrance-design firm.

Ed wanted to know what would happen if we put a regular CD into the disc player. He used the example of "Graceland." Would the room smell like Paul Simon? Elvis's bedroom? The instruction-pamphlet writers at

Scentstories are prepared for people like Ed. Under the WARNINGS section, it actually says: "Only use Scentstories discs in Scentstories player."

The pamphlet writers take a dim view of the American intellect. Users are advised: "Do not drop player. Do not use player upside down." It was as though the device was being marketed to chimps. But only free-range chimps, for the next paragraph said: "Do not use in small confined pet areas without adequate ventilation."

Later in the week, I opened up the box and was met by an alarming and overwhelming smell. I had stored all five scent discs together in the box, with the result that many of the Scentstories had wafted out and blended together. So now the room smelled like Gazing at the Tall Firs Exploring the Mountains Vanilla Nut Cake Comforted with Lavender Vanilla Taffy Relaxing in a Hammock Walking Beside Wildflowers. Ed stopped in on his way to feed the chimps. He sniffed. "Bubblegum paint. I like it."

I Gotta Be . . . You

I never used to worry about identity theft. If you were a thief seeking to get rich and live the high life, becoming Mary Roach was not the way to go about it. You'd have the money to paint the town red, yet you'd be compelled to drive across town to the store that sells paint 50 cents a gallon cheaper. You'd be a thief with an identity crisis.

But lately, owing to a spate of ads and news stories about identity theft, I worry. I recently threw away some ten years of old bank statements and tax forms. In the old days, I'd just toss them. Now, because I noticed that my Social Security number is at the top of every page of my tax forms and many of my old check stubs, I get out a Magic Marker and black them all out.

After about a minute of this, I get bored. The last time, as a distraction, I decided to call up the IRS and let them know they were putting Americans at risk of identity theft.

A man named Jim answered. I suggested to him that they use people's birth dates as an identifier at the top of the forms instead of Social Security numbers.

Jim replied that there are 270 million Americans, and that many of them have the same name and birth date.

"Well, something ought to be done about that too," I said indignantly. "Think about how easy it would be for Peter Smith, 5/13/66, to steal the identity of another Peter Smith, 5/13/66."

Jim was quiet. Maybe he was thinking about it. More likely, he was jotting my name down on IRS Form 498872: Request for Audit of Irksome Journalist. I thanked Jim and went back to my stack of forms and my Magic Marker. To make the time pass more quickly, I pretended I was a World War I counterespionage specialist, censoring troops' letters home lest Allied information fall into enemy hands. Shortly after taps, my husband, Ed, arrived home.

"Good evening, Colonel," I said. It's possible the marker fumes were affecting me. "Something of a backlog here. Looks like I'll be at it till reveille."

Ed blinked. "You're getting black marks on the rug."

Ed doesn't worry about identity theft. He has his own security protocol, which is to cut expired credit cards in two, throw one half away, and put the other half underneath a yellow bowl in the kitchen. "The next time I use the bowl," he explained, "I throw away the other half." I had come across these snippets of plastic and been perplexed. It was as though our house was infested with strange banking squirrels, stockpiling credit for the winter ahead. Financial statements and tax forms aren't a problem for Ed, as he has yet to throw one away.

I decided I needed a paper shredder. I drove over to our local office-supply store, which sold several models. "Did you want the cross cut or the strip cut?" said the salesman, whose identity had obviously been stolen by a butcher. He said he was a fan of the cross-cut model that "turns eight sheets at a time into confetti." Perfect for the Allied victory parade, I thought to myself, adjusting the cuffs on my imaginary uniform.

I was ready to hand him my credit card. Then I stopped. "How do I know you're who you say you are? I can't give you my credit card number. That's top secret information."

"Okay," he said, and turned to the next customer.

I put the paper shredder back on the shelf. In the end, I gave my old tax forms to a friend's fourth-grader, to line the bottom of her hamster cage. If you see a rodent with my name on its checks, let me know.

Furniture Fight

When you move, your head fills with idiotic dreams. You get rid of perfectly good furniture, thinking that when you arrive in your new home you will magically acquire the good taste and cash needed to redecorate. Har.

Last week my husband and I, tired of standing up in front of the TV, found ourselves in a hip, modern furniture store called Design Within Reach. This is a place that sells $3,000 sofas rather than the $10,000 sofas that professional interior designers will reach for. I fell for a three-seater in maroon leather. I motioned to Ed, who was submerged in a chair that resembled the bottom half of a terrifying orange bivalve.

"It's only $3,000," I called. Ed stretched his arm out in the direction of the $3,000 sofa. "I can't reach." As we left, the woman handed me a swatch of the leather, as though perhaps it were possible to grow a sofa from a small cutting.

Ed and I realized that before we could argue about

whether we could afford the sofa, we needed to spend some time arguing about how big it should be and where it was going to go. Ed wanted to line the sofa up alongside an armchair against one wall. This is a distinctly male school of thought as regards living room decor: All large seating items are to be placed against a wall, facing the television. This way, if the lights go out while you are returning from the refrigerator, you need only place one hand upon a wall and begin walking. Eventually you'll hit a place to sit down and nap until the power is back on and the TV is working again.

I pointed out that if three or four people wanted to have a conversation in these seats, they would need to constantly lean forward or back to see around one another's heads. I explained the concept of the "conversation pit," wherein you arrange the sofa and chairs at right angles, so that you can easily see each other while talking. Ed said some disparaging things about women and their endless need to talk, and I replied with an unflattering statement about men and TV-watching. We were in a different kind of conversation pit, the kind the Romans would toss poorly muscled, verbally inclined gladiators into and then watch to see who remained standing.

A few days later, a friend gave us some home décor magazines. These consist of hundreds of pictures of imaginative, tastefully decorated interiors. The pictures are meant to give you ideas for your own home, but mostly they make you feel really, really bad about it. Also, though it isn't written down anywhere, the magazines imply that you will need to clear out all personal belongings except bowls of lemons and vases of artfully arranged twigs. Who are these strange, monklike lemon-eaters? Where are their piles of bills, their overdue videos, their newspapers from last March?

One article suggested cutting out pieces of paper in the dimensions of the furniture we were considering. We could then move these around the floor in different configurations. Ed cut out a sofa, two armchairs, a coffee table. Then he set to work on two more large, square paper cutouts. "Ottomans," explained Ed. "I mean ottomen."

This is a long-standing disagreement between us. I'm a leg-curler-under. Ed is a leg-stretcher-outer. Ed would put an ottoman in front of the toilet if he could. His idea of a winning business venture is to open a store that sells only ottomans and call it The Ottoman Empire.

Two weeks passed. Still we had no furniture. Ed sat down on the paper sofa and patted the space beside him. We lit a fire in the fireplace. In the spirit of compromise, Ed crumpled up a paper ottoman and threw it on the flames. I moved a paper armchair over against the wall. Tomorrow we'd buy some twigs. It was beginning to feel like home.

Can You Hear Me *Now*?

There is a special form of hearing loss that afflicts couples. They don't have to be old, or even middle-aged—just married for a while. Ed's condition is most noticeable when he's reading the newspaper over breakfast. I'll say, for instance, "Oh, look at the cedar waxwings in the birch tree!"

Ed will keep looking at his paper for three or four seconds. Then he'll go: "What did you say?" By now the birds have moved on to the next backyard. Or worse, they'll still be there, forcing me to repeat my inane, mind-numbingly dull comment, a comment not worth repeating to anyone, and in particular, a man transfixed by the latest on Roger Clemens's salary negotiations.

I have come to believe that Ed's hearing loss is also limited to the specific tonal register of my voice. His brain has learned, over time, that this particular vocal range is best ignored because there's a high likelihood it will be a) saying something mind-numbingly dull or b) accusing him of not listening. If someone else—Roger Clemens, for example— were to sit down at our breakfast table and make reference to the cedar waxwings, Ed would look up and respond.

"You bet I would," said Ed when I pointed this out. "You don't take Roger Clemens for granted like you do your wife." He added that there is no such team as the Cedar Waxwings. Then he went back to his paper.

Ed believes that I, too, have a unique form of conjugal hearing loss. I can't make out the first two words of almost anything Ed says to me. I say he mumbles. He says it's me. He printed out a page from a website called Ten Ways to Recognize Hearing Loss. Number 6 said: "Do many people seem to mumble?"

"Not many people," I said. "Just you."

Ed didn't hear this, as he'd walked into the kitchen. This is the other problem with married couples' communications: They attempt to carry them out while standing in separate rooms or on separate floors, preferably while one of them is running water or operating a vacuum cleaner or watching the Cedar Waxwings in the playoffs. Just last night I was at the sink brushing my teeth when Ed responded to something I'd said with the line: "Yours is not to do or die."

"WHO died?" I yelled through the bristles.

"DO OR DIE!!"

"WHO'S DEWAR?"

This is how our conversations go these days. I don't be-lieve it has anything to do with our ears. We're just too lazy to walk down the hall and address each other face to face, like civilized, respectful adults. Ed recently saw a specialist about ringing in his ears, and I went along to get a professional's view on spousal hearing issues.

Dr. Schindler came into the examining room and sat down on his little wheeled stool. He was wearing one of those strapped-on headlamps, for looking down throats or coal mines.

Ed smiled at him. "You have something on your head."

I shook his hand. "I'm here because I have a question about hearing and marriage." Then I launched into the story of how Ed doesn't listen at breakfast, and how he thinks I don't listen when anyone could tell you he's mumbling.

Dr. Schindler said that he wasn't a counselor. The look on his face said, *What part of "otolaryngologist" do you not understand?* Wisely, he did not actually pose this question, or we would all still be there.

Then the doctor began talking about age-related hearing loss. "Around 40, we start to get worse at filtering out background noise . . ." Ed and I are both deep in denial about this so-called "aging" thing. Ed cocked his head toward Dr. Schindler. "Did you say something?"

Cheaper Than Thou

My husband, Ed, once called me the cheapest person in the world. I believe this was around the time he discovered that every night I remove my eyeliner with the end of a Q-tip and then set it aside to use the other end the following night. Ed was appalled. "Do you rinse and reuse your dental floss too?"

I gave him a look of utmost scorn, though it's possible he saw through the scorn to the little light shining behind it, the light that said, "Wow, great idea!"

I know for a fact that I'm not the cheapest person in the world, because it's a matter of record—Guinness record, to be specific—that the world's greatest miser was Hetty Green. And do you know what the *Guinness Book of World Records* cited as evidence of her miserliness? She saved scraps of soap.

And who in our house saves scraps of soap? That would be Ed. When the bar of soap gets so tiny that you can't wash without it crumbling like feta cheese inside your underarms, Ed will take the delicate sliver and fuse it onto the new bar of soap. I can recall the first time I saw this. It was touching in a way, the little infant soap clinging to its mother's back like a baby monkey. The charm wore off over the course of umpteen showers during which the sliver would repeatedly dislodge from its host, forcing me to stand under the water for five minutes at a time fusing it back into place, wasting precious pennies' worth of water—pennies that could be put to good use buying six months' worth of Q-tips.

In Ed's case, it's hereditary. I will always remember the sight of Ed's dad, Bill, eating a salad dressed from a gallon vat of dressing purchased at Costco.

He had bought the largest size because it was the most economical, but as it turned out, he hated the taste of it. Ed encouraged him to throw it away.

"I bought it," he said, chewing miserably, "and I'm going to finish it." This was in 1997. Every time we visit, we check in the refrigerator for the Dressing of Bill's Discontent, marking off his progress in half-inch increments.

We figure his sentence will be up around 2030. We're hoping that he lives that long, first because we love him dearly, and second, because if he doesn't, that means Ed and I will have to bring it home and finish it. Otherwise it would be a waste of perfectly good dressing, "perfectly good" here meaning "not immediately life-threatening." And when the bottom of the evil vat is finally in sight, one of us will turn it upside down, to be sure not a drop goes to waste. We had a honey jar upside down on the breakfast table for the better part of a decade. "Pass the YENOH," Ed would say.

I'd be hard-pressed to say who's more pathetic, Ed or me. We both make ourselves feel better by berating the other person. Ed takes great joy in reminding me of the time a car salesman told me I was the first person he'd ever met who ordered a car with NO extras. I, in turn, take great joy watching Ed rummage through his box of stray, salvaged screws in a predictably hopeless effort to find one that fits.

Yesterday Ed caught me using the Water Miser dishwasher option (I prefer the term Water Conservationist) even though there were dirty, greasy pots inside. I tried to explain that by adding a little extra soap, I could make up the lost cleansing power. Perhaps this might be a good use for those little slivers of bar soap. Ed told me I had a screw loose.

It's possible he's right. And when it falls out, we know where to look for a replacement.

The Grass Menagerie

My father was English, so gardening, I've long assumed, is in my blood, along with gin and fryer grease and a fondness for long, tedious war movies. I recently got a chance to test my theory when we moved to our new house and for the first time in my life I had a yard.

For the first few weeks, I ignored it. Denial is apparently the first stage of gardening. When I finally checked back in on the situation, our lawn had disappeared, the victim of a hostile clover takeover. Ed couldn't see the problem. He pointed out that the clover was coming in thicker and greener than the grass had been. "Let's just mow it and say it's a lawn."

So Ed mowed the clover and the 10 or 20 sad, frightened stalks of lawn grass that the clover were apparently keeping alive as slaves. Presently, he came into the kitchen holding two plastic-and-metal discs at arm's length. "We've got land mines, honey!" Ed had mowed the automatic sprinkler heads.

A yard is not the benign, pretty, passive world it appears to be. It is a war zone. The neighbor's ivy is constantly scaling our fence and attacking on the western front. From the north, dandelions launch airborne spore assaults. Every evening Ed and I meet in the general's tent and plot strategy. Usually I get to be Peter O'Toole, but sometimes Ed makes me be Omar Sharif. "Sir, there's nothing to be done," Ed will say. "They're tunneling under the fence now, coming up from below."

"Bastards." I'll narrow my eyes and set my jaw. "Wire headquarters for more Roundup."

About six weeks into the gardening experience, I noticed that some of our plants were turning brown. "Is this a seasonal thing?" I asked Ed. I had heard of leaves changing color at a certain time of year.

"I think," said Ed gently, "that it's more likely a watering thing."

Watering your plants, I have learned, is not as simple as watering your dog or your car radiator. Not only can you water too little, you can also water too much. To water just right, you must figure out what type of soil you have (brown is not an acceptable answer) and how much shade each area has and how sunny and humid it's been.

But before any of that, you must figure out what type of plants you have. Ed and I have no idea what's growing in our yard, though we give them names anyway. "There's white fuzz growing on the grotticulpis leaves!" I'll shriek.

"And the pifflewort bush has dibblies!" Ed will yell back.

One day I noticed that the trees in our yard had begun dropping dead leaves onto the lawn. "Are we overwatering?" I asked Ed.

"I think," he said gently, "That it's a seasonal thing."

For three solid weeks, it rained leaves. We raked until we had blisters, and dibblies, and blisters on our dibblies. I was fast approaching the third stage of gardening: the calling-in of the professional.

Here's what pushed me over my limit. It was a Saturday afternoon. I was down in the basement failing to understand the sprinkler control console, when I came across a small cabinet crammed with bags and boxes. Organic Bulb Fertilizer, said one label. Azalea and Rhododendron Food, said the next. I looked over at Ed. "What—they *eat* too?" Where would it stop? Would we have to clothe them and drive them to track practice?

So I gave up. As Omar Sharif said in *Lawrence of Arabia*, "Let the English have their gardens. We will make do with barren ground and brittle, unsightly ground cover." Perhaps he didn't say exactly that. But he was thinking it. And I am too.

On the Road Again

A family is a collection of people who share the same genes but cannot agree on a place to pull over for lunch. Ed and I, plus his parents and sister Doris and eight-year-old niece Alisha, are on a road trip to Yosemite. Poppy wants Subway, Ed wants In-N-Out Burger, Mary wants Sonic. In the end, we compromise on McDonalds, where Alisha will get an "Incredibles" action figure that will come in handy later for breaking the heater vent.

We've rented a minivan that seats eight, yet somehow, there are not enough cupholders. How can this be? This is America: To every passenger, a cupholder, and to every cupholder, a watered-down soda big enough to baptize a harbor seal.

"Alisha!" says Doris. "Take Mr. Incredible out of Poppy's cupholder."

It's a three-hour drive to Yosemite, but we're taking a

little longer, as we're working in a tour of Highway 80's public restrooms. As the saying goes, Not one bladder empties, but another fills. I am reminded of that track and field event wherein one person runs for a while, and then hands off the restroom key to the next person, who runs until she's done, and then another person runs.

Unhappily, many of these restrooms belong to gas stations. Gas-station customers, perhaps inspired by the nozzles on the pumps outside, are prone to dribble and slosh. Though I almost prefer this to the high-tech humiliation of air travel, where the restrooms have faucets programmed to respond to precisely executed hand signals no one has taught you, and the toilets flush mere seconds after you sit down. It's like having your plate cleared before you've even salted your potatoes.

We get back on the road. Poppy's driving now. We've entered the road-trip doldrums, the point when all the cheesy tabloids have been read and the travel Etch A Sketch has grown boring, and anyone under age 12 is required to say "Are we there yet?" at ever-shortening intervals. Ed and his sister, two middle-aged adults, are playing with the highway bingo set. Alisha is making Mr. Incredible fight with Poppy's earlobes.

Doris covers the bingo square that says motel. "BINGO!"

"No way," says Ed. "A motel is only one story high and has a swimming pool full of algae. That was a hotel."

"Same diff," says Doris.

"MA! Doris is cheating!"

Alisha kicks the back of Poppy's seat. "Are we there yet?" If by "there" she means the end of our rope, then, yes, we're pulling in right now.

Just outside Manteca, we stop for coffee. Coffee is an important feature of the relay-restroom training regimen. Without it, the chain could be broken, the gold medal lost. At a Starbucks checkout, Ed buys a CD of Joni Mitchell's favorite musical picks. The hope is it will have a calming effect.

The first cut is by Duke Ellington. Alisha makes a face. "Is Uncle Ed trying to annoy us?"

"It's not my favorite Ellington number," agrees Nana. The CD returns to its case, pending the day Joni Mitchell joins us on our annual vacation.

Pulling back onto the highway, it starts to pour, which at least quells the debate over whether to have the windows open. Depending on whom you ask, the temperature inside the minivan is either "freezing" or "so hot I'm going to suffocate."

Then something amazing happens. As we climb the Sierras, the rain turns to snow. The pines are flocked with white. We're struck dumb by the scene outside. For a solid 15 minutes, everyone forgets about their bladder, their blood sugar, the temperature in the van. Alisha has never seen snow, so we pull over to make snow angels and catch falling flakes on our tongues. Then Ed realizes we need tire chains, and we have to turn back and drive 30 miles to Oakhurst.

"Good," says Poppy. "There was a very nice restroom there."

It's Your Fault

We recently moved to a house that lies a quarter-mile from an earthquake fault. For some reason, we did not give this a lot of thought when we bought the place. At the time, the distance from Quick & Juicy Burger or a decent espresso place seemed of greater import. The fault is named Hayward, which may have contributed to our nonchalance, for it makes it sound kindly and avuncular. Prone to tweedy outerwear. Not the sort of name that sends one running for the gas valve.

So we've been reading some of the government's "emergency preparedness" websites to see what we could do to be better prepared.

"Are you ready?" asks the FEMA web page cheerfully, as though a natural disaster were a sort of amusement park ride, and all you need do to survive is be over four feet tall and lower your safety bar. The earthquake page suggests that you "stay in bed" and put a pillow over your head.

It doesn't say to put Lucinda Williams on the stereo and have a good cry, but I think that pretty much goes without saying.

Much space is devoted to the assembly of a home survival kit. This must contain not only the predictable items—water, canned foods—but mysterious items like a pencil and a medicine dropper. Ed mused that the medicine dropper was for nursing baby birds. "They fall from their nests and are unable to locate their parents because all the cell-phone circuits are busy."

"Good," I said. "At least someone will be drinking the canned milk." From here we digressed into a discussion of PET Evaporated Milk. My mother always fed our cats PET milk, and I'd assumed it was a special inexpensive kind of milk for pets. "Why, sure," said Ed. "It's shelved right there next to the IDIOT Milk."

I consulted the website of PET, known to themselves as "the dairy goodness people." Alas, it said that the origins of the name were "lost in history."

The survival kit lists go on for pages. Batteries, sturdy shoes, blankets. I understand the importance of having all these items on hand in your home, but why do you need to drag them from their appointed storage places and put them in a "kit"?

"Because . . . you don't know where anything in your house is even when the electricity is on and the walls aren't falling down?" guessed Ed.

I insisted that I knew where every one of these items was.

"Okay," said Ed. "D batteries?"

I had to admit that the batteries were "lost in history."

"Besides," said Ed. "It's important to have a kit." Ed has a special weakness for kits. We have a first-aid kit in the car and one at home. While packing to move a few months back, I decided to actually look in the home kit. There were three rolls of tape but no bandages. I asked Ed if he planned to tape our wounds shut. He did not answer. I sensed he had other taping-shut plans in his head.

The Department of Homeland Security survival-kit list includes the item "unique family needs." "Chocolate-covered raisins?" said Ed. "Lip gloss," volunteered Phoebe, my stepdaughter.

All the sites stress the importance of having a plan: knowing where to go and what to do. "Stand in a doorway," said Ed. "Get under a desk," said Phoebe. We looked at the FEMA earthquake page. Item 4 said: "Use an interior doorway for shelter only if you know it is a strongly supported, load-bearing doorway." They had forgotten Item 3A: Get an engineering degree.

Ed frowned. "Do I stand in a doorway or not?" I say go for it. Lean against it provocatively while wearing leather slippers and a burgundy dressing gown and say, "Anyone for a nightcap?"

Ed took the Unique Family Needs list and wrote: Scotch.

Taking Its Toll

The highway toll station as a method of tax collection dates to medieval times, long before the existence of postal trucks and other handy means of delivering tax bills to citizens without wasting an hour of their lives every day. Our local bridge district, perhaps staffed by medievalists or those nostalgic for simpler, more irritating times, continues to use a toll plaza.

"Good morrow, sir!" Ed salutes the tax collector as we pass through the gate each morning. His greeting is drowned out by a radio in the booth, or possibly a hurdy-gurdy player in doublet and pantaloons.

To convince commuters they are progress-minded fellows, our bridge district recently installed FasTrak, a system that deducts the toll automatically from your account as you pass. To use it, you send away for a "transponder," which has a promising "Star Trek" ring to it, as if you have only to flip the thing open, press some buttons, and you and your car will vanish, then reappear on the far side of the traffic, wearing form-fitting V-neck uniforms.

In fact, it's just a small, flat beeping plastic box that you put on your dashboard. Some people choose to Velcro the device to their windshield, as a convenience to thieves who can now break your car window, confident that their transgression will, at the very least, produce 20 bucks in bridge tolls.

While FasTrak apparently lives up to its name elsewhere in the nation, our version is not quite there. On our maiden run, traffic was backed up a mile from the toll plaza, the cars all honking and the knights overheating on their caparisoned chargers. Alas, the FasTrak-only lanes begin about 500 yards back from the tollgate, meaning that you can cut, oh, about 35 seconds off your commute. Ed tuned the radio to the 24-hour traffic station. As it was too late to take an alternative route, there was no point in doing this. I didn't say anything, because the day before, Ed had refrained from saying anything when I tried to run my library card through an ATM slot. We do this for each other.

Ed leaned in to the radio speaker, concentrating. "Yup," he said. "Traffic's backed up all along here."

At long last, we neared the FasTrak-only lane. I rummaged in the glove box for the transponder. Ed gave me a queer look, for I had grabbed our Travel Etch A Sketch and set it on the dash. The transponder was in the other car. As it turned out, it didn't much matter. With just two FasTrak-only lanes, both were so clogged that it was actually faster to use a cash lane. To pass the time, I called directory assistance and tracked down the local administrator of the FasTrak program. She had ruined my morning, and now I was going to ruin hers. I asked why there are only two FasTrak-only lanes. And why so short? She said they weren't sure they had the "political stomach for the outcry" from the cash payers that would ensue if more, or longer, FasTrak-only lanes opened up. I gave her some outcry to practice on. Fie upon the cash payers! The goal should be to make these people's commute so miserable that they are forced to get with the program.

"Well," she said. "It's certainly a tough decision. We try to strike a balance and move forward."

"Me too," I said. "I try to move forward too. Oops! Look at that. I can't. Traffic's at a standstill." I hung up the phone.

"Why the hatred?" said Ed. "It's just life." If only I could be like Ed. I decided that from here on out, I would go forward—or maybe just sideways—with acceptance and calm and forgiveness.

As we got to the tollbooth, I smiled and handed the collector an extra dollar. A little something for the hurdy-gurdy man.

A Kiss Is Just . . . a Pain

America is a culture that cannot agree on how to end an evening. Some people are huggers. Some peck, some shake. Ed and I were at a dinner party last week that was particularly treacherous, in that it combined old friends and total strangers, each requiring a different skill set. Ed is better at this, and I turned to him for guidance.

The first to leave was our friend Laurie. "Kisser-hugger," whispered Ed. "No problem there." Her friend Jim was trickier. We'd met him only once, and though I had a dim memory of him as a hugger, I couldn't say for sure what kind. There's full-body frontal, lip/cheek, cheek/cheek, and there's combo. I stepped closer to Jim, imagining a panel of judges off to the side and a team of commentators speaking in hushed tones. "It looks like they're getting ready for a single-side, lateral cheek press with shoulder clasp. That's got a difficulty factor of 5. Let's see how Roach does. In the past she's had trouble with her finish." I pictured them wincing quietly. "That's going to be tough to recover from."

Other cultures have managed to agree upon a national protocol for greetings and farewells, and they simply get on with it. The French kiss each other twice, perhaps because no one else will. The Dutch at some point trumped the French with a triple cheek buss. The English, my people, will step closer and raise their arms to your shoulders while simultaneously leaning away, imparting a vague impression of affection while at the time suggesting it's quite possible they find your kind repellent.

Cross-cultural good-byes are especially trying. I once met a French-Canadian author in an airport and spent a pleasant hour chatting with him. When his flight was called, we stood up to say good-bye. I went for a peck, but because he had turned his head in preparation for a double-cheek press, my mouth collided with the side of his nose. We rushed to make corrections, but it was like trying to steady a plummeting jetliner. The embrace spiraled out of control and crashed to the floor. Black smoke billowing from the departures hall for days.

Cross-generational hugs are also tricky, as I learned with Laurie's mother the other night. A kiss or hug might seem inappropriate, but a handshake might be taken as standoffish.

"Let her make the first move," whispered Ed.

I worried that she might be plotting the same thing. Ed acknowledged that that was a problem, in that we'd both be awkwardly standing there. "High noon in a Clint Eastwood movie" was how he put it.

So I made the first move. I flipped my poncho over one shoulder and removed the cigar. I was going for a cheek/cheek. Though people refer to this as a kiss, it is technically an embrace. It is physically impossible to kiss someone else's cheek while he or she is kissing yours, unless you have highly elastic, protuberant lips. Orangutans can manage the simultaneous cheek kiss, but have the good sense not to bother.

The rest of the table had stood up and begun gathering their coats. We were toward the back of the pack. A man with whom I hadn't exchanged a word was drawing near.

"Hug," Ed whispered urgently. "If you're at the end of the line, and everyone in front of you has been doing the hug, you have no choice. You have to go to the hug."

So I hugged the man, perhaps a bit too exuberantly. He extracted himself as quickly as he could without actually pushing me away. The judges shook their heads sadly.

I can't tell you how happy I was to get home, where the people I love come and go without any of this fuss, unless one of us is heading off for, say, a year in Tripoli. "See ya!" "Bye!" It's so wonderfully simple.

Caught on the Web

Last week I was forced to look myself up on the Internet. I was doing a search on Mary Roach websites, to see if the domain names were taken.

I am not one of those folks who delight in Googling themselves. The last time I succumbed to the urge, the mighty search engine turned up an African wire service story stating that author Mary Roach has "gone off her trolley." I wasn't certain what this meant, or even if it was a bad thing. I mean, who knows, maybe it was my stop? Curious, I then Googled the phrase "off her trolley." I did not find a definition, but I learned that Sharon Osbourne, Ann Coulter and Kate Bush are also off their trolleys. An unpromising sign.

A website, as you know, is a resource designed to provide quick and easy access to outdated or useless information. I give you, for instance, the website Maryroach.net. The Mary Roach in this case is an old *American Idol* contestant whose audition Simon Cowell called one of the worst he'd ever heard. I don't watch *American Idol* very often, but I heard about this Mary Roach, because for two weeks afterward, people in my household were walking around gleefully quoting Cowell's line, "At least we don't have to listen to that horrible MARY ROACH anymore."

Most folks logging onto websites are looking for nothing more than a phone number. But company websites rarely give you one. Why? Because they long ago laid off their phone-answerers in order to hire designers of useless, outdated websites.

In keeping with the general goal of irritating as broadly and efficiently as possible, many websites require passwords. In order to get a password, you must undergo a half hour of tedious, unpaid data entry known as registering. If you've already registered, you can proceed directly to not being able to remember your password, followed by remembering passwords for seven other websites, followed by, as they say in the Good Book, a wailing and gnashing of teeth.

Moving on to www.maryroach.org, I was surprised to find myself redirected to the website of a business called Nature's Drugstore. Here you can buy Eczema Kits, All-Purpose Ointment, and seven different Libido Enhancers, including the eyebrow-elevating "Men's Package." I e-mailed Nature's Drugstore to ask what Mary Roach has to do with all this, but got no reply. There was—Lo!—no phone number, just an address in Greeley, Colorado. Greeley has a website, but there was nothing on it about Nature's

Drugstore. There was, however, a mention of Greeley as the home of "the oldest symphony west of the Mississippi," which may explain all the libido enhancing that's going on there.

You are no doubt wondering why I did not choose www.maryroach.com. The answer is that my online identity has been kidnapped by BuyDomains.com. The ransom has been set, I kid you not, at upwards of $5,000. This is what it would cost to buy back the rights to my name for use with a website ending in dot-com. Simon Cowell did not refer to BuyDomains.com as "the most obnoxious, parasitic, greed-oozing company he'd ever heard of," but who knows, one day he may. If you do a Google search on "irritant," the website of BuyDomains.com pops up. I'm lying. It doesn't. What pops up—true story—is a link to the marketplace eBay: "Great deals on irritant!"

So, for the near future anyway, no one will be able to visit a website belonging to the Mary Roach who does not aspire to a singing career or a cure for eczema.

Dishing Dirt

"It is not necessary to rinse dishes before putting them into the dishwasher." This is line one, page five of our dishwasher's instruction manual. I recited these words to my husband, Ed, last week, so he would understand that it is not just me that holds this opinion, it is also the authors of the Frigidaire Dishwasher Use and Care Manual, and if anyone should have the last word on rinsing, it is these fine people.

And Ed doesn't merely rinse the dishes before putting them in. He all-out washes them—thereby defeating the machine's purpose. If I'd known I could get my husband to wash dishes for me, I wouldn't have insisted we buy a dishwasher. This is a device that washes dishes so that people don't have to, so they have time to go off and pursue their dreams, so they can write the Great American Novel, or the great American Dishwasher Use and Care Manual or whatever it is they dream of writing.

I believe prewashing is demeaning to the dishwasher. If people wash the dishes first, the dishwasher is reduced to a sort of unneeded front-loading autoclave. Imagine the scorn of the other large appliances.

REFRIGERATOR: "So, what do you do around here?"

DISHWASHER: "I make perfectly clean dishes scalding hot for a while."

REFRIGERATOR: "Why on earth would you do that?"

DISHWASHER: "No reason. Utterly pointless. I'm so depressed."

Ed says he rinses the dishes before putting them in because if you don't, they dry out while you wait for a full load to accrue, and then little bits of cereal and egg fuse to the surfaces. True enough. So you don't put the dishes in until you've got a full load; you leave them stacked in the sink with water in them. I acknowledge that there are drawbacks to this method, such as the floating communities of mold and decomposing lunch matter and such that show up after a day or so.

I picked up the Use and Care Manual. Page 10: "Should mold appear on soaking dishes, stop looking in the sink." Ed grabbed the manual from me. Page 16: "If your wife thinks leaving dirty dishes in the sink for days on end is acceptable adult behavior, call our toll-free number and have her committed at absolutely no cost to you."

Ed also believes that the dishwasher is for washing dishes, not pots and pans. He pointed out the drawing in the manual of a properly loaded top rack. In the drawing, the area where I typically wedge frying pans and macaroni dishes is filled with neat rows of dessert plates, cups and saucers. In other words, the entire top half of your dishwasher is reserved for those evenings when the Queen of Norway and her entourage drop in for dinner. Outside of the mold community, we don't get many visitors. Or not the saucer type, anyway. At our house, coffee goes in mugs, and dessert is eaten out of the carton or, in the case of cookies, held in the hand. If the Queen of Norway makes a stink, you serve her her Nutter Butters on a paper towel.

There will be no saucers in my top rack. If I'm going to have a machine help with the dishwashing, I'm going to give the machine all the disgusting, greasy things, and I'll handle the saucers.

Ed and I have reached a compromise, though Ed isn't aware of it yet. Here's how it works. When Ed finds glasses and cereal bowls in the sink, he can go ahead and prewash them and put them in the top rack of the dishwasher. Then, when I need that space for the lasagna pan, I remove the glasses and bowls and put them back in the cupboard. So basically, I have two dishwashers. The Queen of Norway couldn't have it much better.

Suite Dreams

I recently spent a month on a book tour, living out of hotels. Ed, who joined me for a few days, couldn't understand why I'd complain about this. The best thing that could happen to Ed is that each day someone would come to tidy his room and pick the towels up off the floor and change the sheets. You might think that Ed, being married, could count upon his wife for this. Unfortunately for Ed, his wife changes sheets the way other people change the oil. I've got a sticker on the headboard to remind me when four months have gone by. Shortly after Ed and I met, he told me he could see a faint Mary-shaped outline on my bedsheet.

"It's a miracle," I said. "Call the Church! Call the newspapers!"

"Not *that* Mary," said Ed.

Suffice to say, I would not last long as a maid at the Marriott. The chain's founder, J. W. Marriott, believed cleanliness was next to godliness, which possibly explains why there was a copy of his biography alongside the Bible in the bedside-table drawer in my room at the Anchorage Marriott. The book said J.W. would "run his index finger over the furniture, doorsills, and venetian blinds" of his son and daughter-in-law's home. The biographer doesn't mention how long the son and daughter-in-law's marriage lasted, but I'd wager not so very long—two, maybe three changes of the sheets at our house.

Why do I complain about staying in hotels? After all, these were nice hotels, hotels with down comforters and $7 bowls of Cheerios. I guess because it's not home. Nobody's home has a stranger downstairs who calls to wake you each morning even though you always hang up on him. Nobody's home has a wall-mounted hair dryer so loud as to damage your hearing and yet simultaneously so weak as to have no effect on your hair. Nobody's home has a bed with the sheets tucked so tightly that your feet are pressed flat out to the side. Who sleeps like that?

"The ancient Egyptians," said Ed, as he slid in beside me. We lay on our backs, saying unknown things in hieroglyphics.

"Do you want to get the lights?"

"You get the lights." At the last hotel, the lights got me. It took ten minutes to hunt down the switch that controlled the entryway lamp.

Hotel showers are designed by the same sadists who take care of the lamp wiring. Sometimes turning the knob to the left makes the water come out softer. Sometimes it makes it scalding. Some showers deliver a weak drizzle, while others come out as a stinging, gale-force blast. One evening, while soaping my armpits in a Category 3 storm, the shower curtain pulled away from the side of the tub and began billowing like a wet ghost. I'd push it down against the porcelain, and it would pull away again. Water poured onto the floor. Miniature shampoo bottles bobbed in the surf. Suddenly I heard knocking, and a voice I couldn't make out. No doubt the guy from The Weather Channel. "Go away," I said. "No interviews today!" It was the maid. I had to stop her. She would see what I'd done, and punish me by setting the clock radio to go off at 2 a.m.

They do that, you know. They're aware that no one, not even someone with advanced degrees in hotel management such as J. W. Marriott, knows how to work a hotel-room clock radio. You will be forced to yank it from its socket in the middle of the night and hurl it across the room, incurring replacement charges and shame upon checkout. I pushed Casper aside, lunged to the door and locked it. The maid retreated. Then I mopped up the floodwaters and put on my makeup. The hotel had installed special lighting over the mirror that highlighted my eyebags and made me look like Jimmy Carter.

"My fellow Americans," I said kindly. "It is time to address the problem of inconsistent and downright dangerous shower-fixture design." Then I had a $7 bowl of Raisin Bran and went out to flog my book.

And There's the Rub!

The whole spa concept is foreign to me. I don't cleanse my face; I wash it. I don't "release toxins" or parole them or give them time off for good behavior. Even the word "spa" is strange, like the back end of it got left off. Like someone was writing, "I'm off to the spay and neuter clinic," but they collapsed in midsentence, the dog heaving a sigh of relief.

I have set all this aside, however, because I recently got a gift certificate for a local spa and have cajoled my friend Wendy into coming with me for a massage. We are now standing in the room known to ordinary (non-cleansing) people as a locker room. The sign on the door says "Women's Dressing." As though we are salads. Across the hall is the Water Closet. This spa has tried hard to be tony and European, right down to the medical background forms, which request that we "tick" boxes, rather than check them.

The locker room is pristine, and smells like no locker room I've ever been in. The smell turns out to be the lockers themselves: They're lined with cedar. "Check, I mean tick, this out," I tell Wendy. "In case moths attack while we're off getting our massages."

A beautiful young attendant arrives to show us how to operate the locks on the lockers. Then she leaves to get us bathrobes and towels.

Wendy looks stressed. "Do we have to tip her for this? I hate these places. I don't know how to behave. What do I tip? Do I take everything off? Do I leave on my underwear?" Wendy is going to need a second massage to relieve the stress that's accumulated while being here for the first one.

We are told to wait for our masseuses in the lounge. It's a gorgeous, perfect lounge with expensive cheeses and orchids and pitchers of lemon water. We pour ourselves some water and finish our medical forms. Wendy is reading aloud: "Are you pregnant? Ha! No, I just look like it!"

A different beautiful young attendant comes into the lounge to refill the water pitcher and clear away the empty glasses. She glances briefly at the flabby, wrinkly things on the sofa, as if giving thought to how she might clear those away too.

At last our masseuses arrive to take us to the treatment rooms. I watch Wendy disappear down the hallway, her voice trailing off: "I left my underwear on. Was that bad? I wasn't sure . . ."

My masseur, Leo, tells me to "disrobe to my level of comfort" and get under the sheet on the massage table. Then he leaves the room. I notice that a small pink flower is lying on the sheet at the head of the massage table, as though the last person was a shrub. The massage table is outfitted at one end with a small, heavily padded toilet seat. When he returns, Leo tells me to put my face inside the toilet seat, which he calls a "face cradle."

Leo says he'll be "opening up my muscles" and "getting blood into the area." This doesn't sound relaxing. It sounds like the tiger scene in *Gladiator.* I bury my face in the toilet and pray for leniency.

Eventually I relax. Things are going swell. Then Leo asks me if I want the "complimentary parafango treatment." There are so many things I need to learn before I can answer this question.

"Fango means volcanic," Leo adds, bringing me no closer to a decision.

"Oh," I say. "In what language?"

He doesn't answer. He must think I'm testing him. For the next few minutes, Leo gives me the complimentary silent treatment. This is fine with me. In my experience, conversations in which one party has her head in the toilet bowl are always trying.

I find Wendy waiting for me in the lounge. She got the parafango treatment on her feet. "And how was that?" I ask her.

"Really relaxing," she says in a strangled voice that I have heard her use only once before, when raccoons got into the compost. "Can we go now?" Wendy gets up and moves toward the door very fast, faster than you would expect for someone whose feet have been dipped in molten magma.

Nivea Man

Men are moisturizing, and I'm a little concerned. One of the things men have always done best is not waste money on personal grooming. You could depend on a man not to slap down a day's pay for a thimbleful of "age-defying" face goo. Men wash their faces with soap, and then—provided there's a towel or curtain hem handy—they dry it. This is the male skin-care regimen in its entirety.

Now men are starting to question themselves. My own husband recently said to me, "Should I be moisturizing my face?" We were in The Body Shop, which now has a "For Men" line of skin care. This includes a moisturizer that they have named Face Protector, no doubt an attempt to make male customers feel more comfortable by evoking a familiar sports-gear image.

The concept of moisturizer is confusing to men, because the traditional male moisturizer has nothing to do with wrinkles. This is a substance that comes in plastic tubs, like spackling compound or bait, and has manly names like Mariner's Hand Cream and No-Crack Hand Healer. The idea is that you've been out in the elements, doing rough, masculine things, and your hands are calloused and chapped and cracked. Your hands, like your saddle or your rifle stock, are simply practical objects that need oiling now and again. Nothing sissy about it.

Since few men repair crankshafts or build docks with their faces, the male had no need for a facial moisturizer. Indeed, they are hazy on the concept. Ed asked me if he should use my Nivea Creme on his face. "That's hand lotion," I said. To a woman, this is like, I don't know, shampooing with dishwashing soap, which I have seen a man do, yes I have.

"You can't use hand lotion on your face?" Ed looked flummoxed. I explained that while hand lotion is for dryness and chapping, facial moisturizer is for softening and reducing fine lines. He pointed to the parentheses on either side of his mouth. "Will it get rid of these?"

Those aren't fine lines, I told him; those are deep grooves. There's a fine line between explaining and insulting, and I had just reduced it. Ed stomped from the room, though the drama of his exit was marred somewhat by his having to rush about and paw through his affairs for his cell phone, wallet, car keys, sunglasses, and ChapStick.

Today's men badly need purses, but here they're resisting the urban trend toward girlification. Like many a modern male, Ed has taken to wearing his camera and cell phone on his belt. The belt has become a sort of contemporary holster, blending practicality and frontier masculinity. Hold it right there, pardner, I've got a call coming in.

Eventually, Ed left the room. He walked out the door with a wide, confident stride, a manly swagger that said, I'm gonna go mend some barbed wire. Maybe fix a crankshaft with my face. And when I get back, woman, you best have my exfoliant ready.

Grape Expectations

When Ed's parents visit, we try to take them to someplace new and different. Since they don't drink or even especially like wine, we felt confident a wine-tasting trip to Napa Valley would fit the bill.

Ed's parents are in their 80s now, so pretty much any option that ends in "ing," you can bet they would secretly prefer to skip. This includes paddle-boating, tandem bike-riding, and a host of other activities they have gamely submitted to, all the while dreaming of Scrabble or a nap in the sun. I don't know why grown children do this to parents. When Bill and Jeanne aren't visiting us, Ed and I are content to spend weekends lolling around reading the paper, napping in the sun, playing Scrabble. The outings, I suspect, are an attempt to convince them that our lives are fascinating and fulfilling.

Ed and I aren't the kind of people who taste wines because they plan to actually buy some of them. But thank

God for these people, because the money they spend helps wineries recover from the huge amounts they lose on people like us. We go wine tasting because it's free.

Things started off swell, because the first winery we stopped at had food tasting too. There were cheeses, olives and pâtés everywhere you turned. Ed made straight for a roasted-garlic olive oil. Bread had been cut into slivers, to make it clear that you were tasting here, not having lunch. This did not deter Ed.

"Wow," he said. "Taste this olive oil again and again and again."

Here is one of the great things about America, possibly the best thing. No one cares if you take five free samples. This is not true in, say, Tokyo. Japan subscribes to a strict moral code regarding the sampling of wares. I didn't realize this when I was there some years ago with a friend. We had figured out that an affordable early supper could be had by working a circuit of the food section of any major department store. By the third circuit, they were onto us. They'd see us coming and rush over to pull away the sample tray, like peasants scrambling to hide their daughters from marauding Huns.

In the next room, the wine staff was pouring tastes of five wines at the bar. Every few feet was a small bucket, and some fellow tasters were pouring out their samples into the bucket after the first sip.

"That seems rude," said Jeanne.

"And wasteful," said Bill. We all nodded and drained our glasses.

As we sampled the next wine, Bill divulged that he and Jeanne had once taken a class on wines. Ed was shocked. "Dad, the last time you were at our house, Mom put a red wine in the refrigerator."

Jeanne stepped back in mock horror. "Oh, my God, what's wrong with me!"

Bill defended her. "You want it to be cold. That way you can't taste it as much." I asked what they'd learned about wine. Bill thought a moment. "Some of it's red, some white."

Jeanne nodded thoughtfully. "And some of it is in between." They were in fine spirits. We all were. We were on the fourth wine by now.

The last one was a Cabernet. "This one has more body," the winery woman told Bill.

"That's okay," said Bill. "If you look at me, I have more body too." Then he announced the Cabernet had "legs." He was swirling his glass like a cowboy with a lasso. The liquid rose dangerously close to the rim, then receded. "See? When it sticks to the glass and hangs down like this, it means, ah . . ." He looked at Jeanne, who stepped right in: "It means that it hangs down more."

They're quite a team, Bill and Jeanne. I said the two of them, together, are like a fine French Bordeaux. What I meant is that their love continues to grow and mellow with age. I did not mean anything about preferring to lie down a lot in a darkened room. They knew what I meant. They gave me a hug, and we drank a toast to the day, to each other, to love, to free wine.

Sit Back and Relax

There is a special room in hell where the flames are extra hot and you must sleep sitting straight up. The sign on the door says: Reserved for People Who Reclined Their Seatbacks the Entire Flight. Most of us understand the discomfort we are inflicting on the poor schmo behind us and try to limit our reclining for the lights-out portion of the flight. If everyone leans back together, in the manner of a synchronized, unattractively upholstered Esther Williams swim routine, then no one is unfairly crowded.

I had a seatback diva in front of me last week. We were barely airborne, and there she was in my lap. Using my computer would now entail making a slit in my belly flab and inserting the front half of the keyboard inside me, so that the bottom row of letters were rendered inaccessible and I would have to make do without the words *banana, vixen, balaclava* and many other colorful favorites.

Defeated, I tried to watch the little TV mounted in the

seatback in front of me. Alas, the screen was so close to my face that my eyes were crossing. Emeril had become a set of perfectly choreographed twin Emerils, which was one or possibly two more Emerils than I could handle. In desperation, I turned to my complimentary copy of the *Sky Mall* catalog and began to read. A mail-order company was selling "the Most Compact Washing Machine in the World," enabling, I don't know, Keebler elves to do laundry in their tree. "Tiki Head Tissue Box Dispenses Tissue Through the Nose!" another ad reported excitedly.

"Who would buy this?" I said to the man in the middle seat, but he was busy waving down a flight attendant. "Miss?" He was holding up his knees. "Is there room in the overhead bin for these?"

We hit a pocket of turbulence and Bloody Mary mix slopped onto the chinos of the man next to me. I pointed to the Most Compact Washing Machine in the World. "You need this," I said. The man did not smile. His expression was just like the Tiki Head with tissues up its nostrils, displeased and clearly embarrassed about the situation yet resolutely stoic.

More and more, you must board a plane like a general going to war. You must constantly defend your turf—your wee, airless kingdom. The occupier of the next seat will make his move upon your armrest the moment your vigilance flags. You will return from the bathroom to find an elbow planted in the little vinyl peninsula where your people once roamed free.

The battle for armrest dominance has grown ever more

intense in the era of the laptop computer. The airplane seat—designed to be a chair, and never very good at it—has now been asked to perform double duty as an office. Soon people will be bringing fitness equipment and hobby craft aboard, and the company that makes the elfin washers will need to get started on looms and rowing machines.

Complex rules apply to the space beneath your seat, for it belongs, technically, to the person behind you. Not long ago, I was on a transcontinental flight when I was awakened by the woman behind me. "Excuse me?" She was holding a plastic juice cup. "Excuse me? This is coming in my section." I had put my empty cup under my seat and it had slid backward, crossing an imaginary line in the carpeting. She was peeved. Her eyes were squinty and her nostrils were flaring, as though about to dispense tissues through the nose.

People were staring, so I took the cup. Later that night, a pantyhosed foot made a stealth assault on the back of my right armrest. It was her: the Juice Cup Border Patrol.

"Excuse me?" I nudged the foot ungently. "This is coming in my section."

Several hours went by without incident. I was beginning to drift off, when I heard a driving, tinny noise: *ch-ch, ch-ch, ch-ch, ch-ch* . . . The woman behind me had mobilized the most fearsome weapon in the modern airplane arsenal: the Overly Loud Headphones.

I waved my hot towel in surrender.

Sleepless in Suburbia

Though I have always been a sound sleeper, I am frequently up at 4 a.m. This is around the time that my husband, Ed, having woken up at 3, will generally crawl back into bed. Ed goes downstairs to watch TV so that his tossing and turning doesn't wake me up. This is very considerate, except that when he returns, he likes to chat about what he's been watching. The other night, Ed had been watching an infomercial for something called the Steam Shark. I have a distinct memory of surfacing from the depths of sleep directly into the sentence "You can steam-clean around the base of the toilet."

Last night it was "Honey, Bo Schembechler died."

Schembechler, Ed explained to my inert self, was a beloved University of Michigan football coach. There is little difference between talking to me about college football when I'm asleep and talking to me about it when I'm awake. Eyelid position, basically, is the difference. Ed kept going: "He was the voice of the Wolverines."

I was partly awake at this point, and for some reason, the sentence struck me as the funniest thing I'd heard in a very long time. Different rules apply between the hours of 2 and 4 a.m., I find. Things that would ordinarily not even qualify as mildly amusing will often, at 3 a.m., strike the ear as high comedy.

Worries are similarly warped. I recently spent the hour from 4 to 5 a.m. worrying about the placement of two shrubs we had planted in our yard that day. Ed came in from downstairs, and I unloaded my fears about the overly close positioning of the shrubbery. I made him promise that first thing the next day, we would dig one up and move it, lest they crowd each other's roots. In the morning, we went out to look at the plants. If anything, they looked a little lonesome there at 17 inches apart, just as the label had recommended. I am now known far and wide as the Nervous Gardener.

Anyway, once the laughter sets in, we're both up. The topic of wolverines led to savage animals in general, and from there to a game called African Veldt. We frequently make up mindless games to wile away the time until the sandman agrees to take over the proceedings again.

"First person to run out of animals is the loser," I said. Ed pointed out that since I had been to Africa, the game was rigged in my favor. He made me name three animals for every one of his.

"Fine. Leopard, zebra, elephant."

"Lion," said Ed with great confidence.

"Warthog, wildebeest, springbok."

A long time went by. The shrubbery roots were closing in upon each other. Finally, and with great hesitancy, Ed said, "Giraffe?"

"Eland, gnu, ostrich."

"You can't do birds."

"Birds are animals."

"Okay, ant," said Ed, and then he rolled over. He took his bottom pillow and put it on top of his head. This is known as the Ed sandwich: pillow, Ed's head, pillow. He does this because he can't sleep if there's noise in the room. There isn't now, but there will be. I make noises while I sleep, and Ed has had many hours to devote to cataloging them. Common varietals include the Click, the Tommy gun and the Darth Vader.

Light is also a problem for my husband. There can be no light in the bedroom, not even the light from the digital clock, which is hidden away on the bottom shelf of Ed's nightstand, broadcasting the time to toddlers and gnomes. The room across the hall must also be dark. We can't just close our bedroom door to block the light from that room, because this will make the bedroom too stuffy for Ed to sleep. That room must also have its curtains drawn. If he could, Ed would draw the curtains on the windows of our neighbors across the driveway, and on down the street, all the way to the horizon.

Kitchen Confidential

I have certain expectations for a kitchen item that costs more than $300. I expect it to have a motor and a plug and a lengthy instruction booklet that I will fail to read, causing an incident wherein an improperly secured part dislodges itself, allowing food matter to be sprayed evenly and efficiently across vertical kitchen surfaces including the cook and a guest and the guest's cashmere sweater set.

So when my husband, Ed, announced he wanted to buy a pot—a pot—that costs $345, he encountered some resistance. Perhaps he had been anticipating this, for he did not refer to the pot as a "pot," but rather as a "seven-quart pasta pentola." He may also have pronounced "quart" as "carat," hoping to appeal to some perceived female gem lust.

A pentola, apparently, is a pot with a matching colander that fits inside it. It is the cashmere sweater set of cookery. I pointed out that we already have a very nice colander.

"But this way, you just lift out the colander," said Ed.

"You don't have to pour the pasta water into the sink." Ed drew out the word *pour,* so it sounded like an elaborate or somehow heroic undertaking.

"But at some point," I said gently, "you will need to pour the pasta water into the sink, correct? Unless you plan to throw the pot away after using it once. If you're the kind of person who spends $345 on a pot for boiling water, I suppose it's a short trip to being the sort of person who throws a pot away after each use."

Ed hesitated. I could tell he was cooking up a story, and no doubt there is a special $350 pot for this too. He tried to convince me that pouring boiling water down the drain could "melt the caulk." I knew this to be a bluff. Otherwise, the drain cleaner people would not instruct you to pour boiling water down the sink before you pour in the drain cleaner. And if you can't trust the drain cleaner people, whom in this world can you trust?

Ed shifted tactics. He began explaining the various high-tech virtues of this brand of pot, which was called All-Clad Stainless. The name refers to a process whereby steel outer layers are bonded to an inner core of aluminum. This way, you have the benefits of stainless steel, which is pretty and durable, as well as the benefits of aluminum, which is neither but redeems itself by heating up quickly and evenly. "So you get uniform heating," said Ed learnedly.

This made sense, except that we were talking about boiling water. "So, the idea is to make sure the boiling water in one half of the pot isn't hotter than the boiling water on the other side?"

Ed was humming to himself. "I can't hear you."

Later, I read on the Web that the All-Clad "molecular bonding" process was developed by NASA.

The man who answered the NASA telephone had not heard of All-Clad. His name was Bill. I asked him how the astronauts make pasta. Bill said they put the pasta pouch into a warmer. "Then they take scissors and cut it open and eat out of the package." These were my kind of people.

To make Ed feel excessive and wasteful, I told him the sum total of the cookware on board the space station is a warmer and a pair of scissors. Then I felt bad. Because what it came down to was that Ed simply wanted a decent pasta pot with a lid that fits. The one we have came without a lid. It was an All-Clad that Ed had got half price, thinking he could order a lid to fit it. And the reason he bought this half-price, lidless pot in the first place was to avoid arguing with his harpy of a wife, who is reliably, pointlessly, tediously cheap. When Ed called to order the lid, he was told they did not make a lid for this pot. "It was an experimental pot," the woman said enigmatically.

In the end, we compromised. We bought a nice, new pot with a lid that fits, and made do without the cashmere colander insert.

Best Cheap Fun!

The price of a movie has gone double-digit. You need a major-league contract to afford an afternoon at the ballpark. Has fun priced itself out of our lives? Not at all.

- *Photo booths.* While you wait for your strip to be developed, reach up and feel around the top of the booth. People often toss their embarrassing outtakes up there.

- *Bubble Wrap*

- *Your cat.* Blow into his face. Stick your finger in his mouth as he yawns. Put him on a leash and try to take him for a walk.

- *The sight of a dog wearing one of those medical lamp shades on its head.* For immediate gratification, do a Google image search for "Elizabethan collar," which is what veterinarians call it.

- *Wave at people while you drive.*

- *Helium Balloons*

- *The weekly police roundup in any small-town newspaper.* I am still laughing over the report of a man seen running naked down a neighborhood street. A policeman who arrived to investigate noticed a note on a car windshield that read "Gone to get parts." The officer misread this as "Gone to get pants" and, satisfied that this explained the man's nudity, returned to his beat.

- *Bumper Cars*

- *The commuter ferry on a blustery day.* My brother comes to visit me once a year, and if the weather's dramatic, we always head for the ferry dock. Go on the weekend and have the ship to yourself.

- *Order a dish off the Chinese-language side of the menu.*

- *Attempt to sneak a bottle of water onto the plane.*

- *Come visit me in jail after someone from Homeland Security reads the above.*

- *Any toenail polish color besides red.*

- *Bubblegum*

- *Type "yink" into your spell checker and read the suggestions out loud.*

- *Those 25-cent horsy rides outside the Walmart.*

- *Root for the Red Sox at Yankee Stadium.*

- *Request a phony page on the White Courtesy Telephone I once heard (in a hospital) "Al Bumin, dial operator. Al Bumin, operator please."* Someone in my dorm in London once paged "Mahatma Coat.

- *Did you know there's a brand of dishwashing detergent in Iran called Barf? Or that Japan sells a sports drink called Pocari Sweat?*

- *Supermarkets in foreign countries.*

- *Launch a message in a bottle with your e-mail address.* For maximum exoticism of response, remember to do it when the tide is going out, not coming in.

- *Lie down in a cow pasture.* If the herd is far off, yell to get their attention, then immediately drop down and lie flat. The entire herd will come galloping over and form a tight circle around you, staring down at you with intense bovine curiosity. I have tried this three times on two different continents. It's marvelously surreal.

- *Late Night Infomercials*

- *Armpit farts.* Here's a variation that will make you feel less childish (but fools no one). It works best in humid weather. Lie on a wood floor, pull up your shirt and press your slightly damp lower back into the floor as firmly as you can. Then pull away quickly. This is also a good lower-back strengthening exercise, but who cares.

1-800-WasteMyTime

It was late in the afternoon, and I was putting the final burnishes on a piece of writing that I was feeling pretty good about. Yes, okay, it was an e-mail, but it was a clever one and I hated to lose it. My cursor had frozen. I tried to shut the computer down, and it seized up altogether. Unsure of what else to do, I yanked the battery out.

Unfortunately, Windows had been in the midst of a delicate and crucial undertaking. The next morning, when I turned my computer back on, it informed me that a file had been corrupted and Windows would not load. This was followed by some mysterious lines of code, which I took to be my computer saying, "Serves you right, careless pea brain," in its native tongue. More graciously, it offered to repair itself by using the Windows Setup CD.

I opened the special drawer where I keep CDs that I have no intention of ever using. There was an IKEA how-to CD, which featured young Swedes assembling kitchen cabinets with nothing but a sardine can key and untrammeled wholesomeness. Mostly, there were CDs of music that my friends are always burning for me, unbidden, because they think I'll enjoy them.

But no Windows CD. I was forced to call the computer company's Global Support Center. My call was answered by a woman in some unnamed, far-off land. I find it vexing to make small talk with someone when I don't know what continent they're standing on. Suppose I were to comment on the beautiful weather we've been having when there was a monsoon at the other end of the phone? So I got right to the point.

"My computer is telling me a file is corrupted and it wants to fix itself, but I don't have the Windows Setup CD."

"So you're having a problem with your Windows Setup CD." She had apparently been dozing and, having come to just as the sentence ended, was attempting to cover for her inattention. I recognized the technique from a thousand breakfast conversations.

"We took that rug in weeks ago. Should I call the cleaners?"

"No, thanks. I'm good."

It quickly became clear that the woman was not a computer technician. Her job was to serve as a gatekeeper, a human shield for the techs, who were off in the back room, or possibly another far-off continent, playing cards and burning CDs for their friends. Her sole duty, as far as I could tell, was to raise global stress levels.

To make me disappear, the woman gave me the phone

number for Windows' creator, Microsoft. This is like giving someone the phone number for, I don't know, North America. Besides, the CD worked; I just didn't have it. No matter how many times I repeated my story, we came back to the same place. She was unflappable and resolutely polite.

When my voice hit a certain decibel, I was passed along, like a hot, irritable potato, to a technician.

"You don't have the Windows Setup CD, ma'am, because you don't need it," he explained cheerfully. "Windows came preinstalled on your computer!"

"But I do need it."

"Yes, but you don't have it."

We went on like this for a while. Finally, he offered to walk me through the use of a different CD, one that would erase my entire system. "Of course, you'd lose all your e-mail, your documents, your photos." It was like offering to drop a safe on my head to cure my headache. "You might be able to recover them, but it would be expensive." He sounded delighted. "And it's not covered by the warranty!" The safe began to seem like a good idea, provided it was full.

I hung up the phone and drove my computer to a small, friendly repair place I'd heard about. A smart, helpful man dug out a Windows CD and told me it wouldn't be a problem. An hour later, he called to let me know it was ready. I thanked him, and we chatted about the weather, which was the same outside my window as it was outside his.

Dinner Party Debt

Our friend Dave loves to cook. Dave will call us up and say, "Hey, come on over. I got a leg of lamb," as though it had just sort of landed in his lap like a fly ball. Dave talks very fast, which he needs to do to answer the question "What're you making?" in a reasonable amount of time. The last time we went to Dave's—for a 50th birthday dinner for our friend Sandy—the answer was, and I'm not even slightly kidding here, "Gonna start with oysters with lemongrass and a blood orange granité, then a fish plate with halibut and preserved lemon, a little cauliflower soup, pasta with anchovy sauce. Meat course, I'm thinking bavette steak with white beans and fennel. Ed eats beef, right? If not, I'll whip him up some Thai snapper."

We happen to have a Thai cookbook, which we use constantly (for propping up the Tex-Mex cookbook), and it has a recipe for snapper. So I happen to know this isn't something you "whip up." It is something that whips you. The shopping alone would require a month's sabbatical. The recipe called for, among 278 other ingredients, "1 tablespoon coarsely chopped kha." As I know from our Scrabble dictionary, ka is what the ancient Egyptians called the soul. Who sells this? What sort of knife does one use to chop life energy?

Generosity like Dave's is difficult to reciprocate. I once tried to cook for Dave and Kate. It was humiliating. I made angel hair pasta with toasted walnuts and some variety of cheese that had not showered in a while. When I tried to mix everything together, the angel hair pasta simply moved around the bowl in a solid lumpen knot. "You forgot the conditioner," said Ed, who has since quietly absorbed the cooking duties on the rare evenings when we're not eating at Dave's.

I have tried to convince myself it's okay that Ed and I have not properly reciprocated by preparing 22 six-course dinners for Dave and Kate. "He understands that we're not up to it," I said to Ed. "Besides, he's not keeping score."

"Everyone keeps score," said Ed. "How many times have we had Lou over without his inviting us?" Lou is one of a small group of bachelors whom we sometimes invite over for a meal at the last minute. It is never intimidating to cook for these men, as your culinary talents need only surpass those of Mr. Top and his ramen.

But Ed was right. I knew exactly how many times Lou had been over.

Last week I e-mailed Dave to tell him I'm writing a column about dinner party debt. Dave was leaving on a business trip that afternoon. "Have a good trip," I wrote. "When you get back, you'll be eating at our house for the next year and a half." I had anticipated some reassuring reply, something along the lines of: "Oh, Mary, I cook for you guys because I love to cook, and I love you. In fact, what are you doing next Saturday? I got a school of tuna."

However, Dave wrote: "Gotta run. Look forward to collecting."

It's true. Everyone keeps track. We owe Dave, we owe Steph and Jerry, we owe Bill and Adair big time. We actually sat down and made a list. It was shocking. "What should we do?" said Ed. Can we offer them the cash equivalency? How can we ever erase such an enormous pile of debt? Is it possible to declare dinner party bankruptcy? There should be a system in place that allows us to collect credits for feeding Lou, credits that we can then apply to Dave and Bill and Steph.

If I could, I would sell Dave my soul to repay his kindness and generosity. And I know for sure that he's got the right knife to chop it up.

Garbage Gone Wild

One day last year, our progressive California city distributed small green plastic compost bins designed to collect kitchen scraps and create marital disharmony. While I was eager to contribute to the municipal composting effort, my husband, being the hygienic sort, was less so. He ignored the little green bin, which was not, after a while, easy to do. Owing to my failure to empty the little bin into its bigger counterpart each Monday when the trashmen came, what was going on inside was not composting, but garden-variety rotting and stinking.

Ed banished the bin to the deck. Now that I couldn't smell it, I would forget about it for weeks on end. The city was not so much composting as creating subsidized housing for molds and flies and their little squirming children.

One day I saw Ed coming up the driveway holding, at arm's length, what we had come to call the maggot zoo. He was approaching the trio of wheeled garbage, recycling and compost-toter bins lined up alongside our house. "Which bin do you use for bins?" he said.

So we went back to our old ways: Ed using the in-sink Disposall, and me, having heard this was bad for our waterways, scraping the plates into the kitchen trash. Then we came upon a product called the Touchless Trashcan. Its lid had an "infrared sensor eye" that enabled it to sense your approaching hand and automatically open for you. "It is convenient to use, and it is very hygienic," said the packaging. We succumbed.

The Touchless Trashcan came in three pieces and included a four-page user manual. One piece, the enigmatic Smart Retainer Ring, required eight steps to install and took up an entire page of the manual. The page was captioned "How Does Smart Retainer Ring Work?" The first thing to hit the bottom of our new can was the user manual. "I refuse," said Ed, "to read a garbage can instruction manual."

The Retainer Ring, we finally figured out, had nothing to do with the automatic lid opener. Its purpose was to prevent the top of the bag from sticking out in an unsightly manner. And also to turn the task of changing the garbage bag into a ten-minute ordeal involving, quoting Ed, "an engineering degree from Rensselaer Polytechnic."

Ed stuck a bag into the can, folded its top over the edge in the usual way and dangled the Smart Retainer Ring over the can. "Oops. I inadvertently threw the Smart Retainer Ring away."

We lowered the automated top onto the bin and

switched on the infrared sensor eye. For three or four minutes, throwing things away was a delightful novelty.

Like many infatuations, that of a touchless trash can and its owners soon sours. For us, it happened that night after dinner. The sensor eye couldn't see very far, and so the lid tended to pop open at the last second, knocking garbage out of your hand and to the floor. I understood why this was happening, but it came across as impertinence. Also, since the eye didn't sense garbage per se but rather the heat of your hand, it ignored things like platters and dustpans. Ed came in one day to see me moving the dustpan over the lid in a series of slow, priestly motions, a ritual that became known as "the blessing of the refuse."

Some weeks later, the touchless can took to intermittently popping open its lid when one of us passed by. Sometimes I'd catch Ed standing there, staring at it. "What does it want?" he'd say.

I had a different interpretation. "It's trying to imply that you and I are garbage."

Ed didn't believe this. "Maybe it just wants to be touched." Owing to the number of times it had slapped fish heads or yogurt lids out of my hand, its top and sides were spattered with food yuck, and neither of us was willing to test Ed's theory and embrace Touchless Trashcan.

In the end, the automated touchless trash can was replaced by the old-fashioned kind of touchless trash can—the kind that opens with a foot pedal. It requires no batteries, and if it has an opinion about its owners, it keeps it to itself.

Alarming Events

Last month, upon hearing that a neighbor had been burgled, my husband voiced a desire to beef up our home security. I was largely unresponsive. It's hard for me to feel threatened by a verb that is one letter off from *gurgle*. The previous owners of our house installed a burglar alarm system, but we never got it switched on, because, quoting Ed, I apparently care more about the $29 monthly fee than I do about our family heirlooms. I gave in, even though I question the likelihood of strangers risking jail time for my father's brass-plated Lions Club paperweight or Ed's mom's blondie recipe. (Though that is only because they haven't tried his mom's blondies.)

The alarm company sent over a sales representative, a well-coiffed professional in a suit and heels. She recommended adding some infrared motion sensors. I was not wild about this. I like to keep things simple. My idea of home security is to hire cheap, disreputable painters who can be counted upon to paint the windows shut. "Besides, can't the motion sensors be set off by a pet?" I said.

Ed leaned in close to the sales rep. "We don't have any pets," he whispered. The sales rep looked me over: the sweatpants, the Goofy slippers, the unbrushed hair. You could tell I was fitting right in with her mental image of People With Imaginary Pets.

"We don't have a pet *now*," I conceded. "But we might someday." I knew this to be a lie. Ed is a dog person, and I'm a cat person. We cancel each other out. Though sometimes I let Ed take the slippers for a walk.

I pointed out that every now and then, the neighbors' cat, Sprinkles, who likes to sleep on our deck, will sneak into the house when the back door is open. The alarm woman started talking about "pet resistance." This was a feature of the motion sensor whereby it was set to cover the room from the waist up only. "Though of course . . ." She hesitated. "The cat would have to stay on the ground at all times." She did not verbalize the logical follow-up: "So you'll want to induce a coma before heading out for the evening."

We got the sensors, and we got the system switched on. We never got a pet, each of us practicing his or her own particular brand of pet resistance, but we did, after many years of cost-based bickering, get a housecleaner. Here we compromised by having her come less often than normal people's cleaners. Every other month, Natalia can be seen machete-ing her way through the filth and cobwebs. I gave her the alarm code but promised to leave the alarm off the day she came.

Naturally, I forgot. Later that morning, my work phone rang. It was Natalia, yelling in harmony with the shrieking of the alarm. She couldn't find the code. On top of all this, my cell phone started ringing. This was the alarm company, responding to the alarm and calling me to get the secret password—which was different from the shutoff code—required for them to shut off the system and prevent the police from rushing over to arrest Natalia for breaking and entering. The machete was bound to complicate her defense.

Some weeks back, Ed and I had spent 15 minutes arguing over the secret password for the alarm. Ed is a fan of the complicated, hacker-proof, identity-theft-foiling password, the kind that involves alternating capital and lowercase letters with obscure foreign accent marks, interspersed with the square roots of street numbers from 35 years ago. Whereas I'll use my name. I had no recollection of what we'd settled on. "Ummmm." The alarm, and Natalia, continued to go off.

The alarm lady gave me a hint, as a game show host will do from time to time out of pity for a contestant who is bombing unbearably. "Begins with *G*." "Groach? Goofy?" This went on for some time. Meanwhile, Natalia had dug through her bag, found the piece of paper I'd given her with the shutoff code and quieted the screaming alarm. I don't know how effective these alarms are against burglars, but Sprinkles hasn't been seen on the property in weeks.

RV There Yet?

An RV is a very, very big vehicle, except when you are inside it with your husband Ed, his daughters Lily and Phoebe, his sister Doris and her ten-year-old Alisha, and your in-laws. Then it is very, very small. RVs are interesting that way.

We are headed for the Grand Canyon, taking the route of a family road trip 40 years ago, when Ed and his sister were about Alisha's age and 31-foot RVs were just a twinkle in a madman's eye. The RV, which we rented in Las Vegas, was Doris's idea. "It's just like a regular car," she assured us. "Only long."

Ed is trying to maneuver out of the RV parking lot. This is not easy to do when the rear of your vehicle is in Las Vegas and the front is already pulling into the Grand Canyon Visitor Center. Ed's mom puts a hand on his shoulder. "How you doing?"

"Great," says Ed, without unclenching his jaw. "It's really fun."

An hour out, just past Hoover Dam, Ed finally begins to relax, and a tire blows. He pulls into a parking lot, and a bunch of us pile out to look at the damage. A piece of rubber the size of a playing card has been ripped from the tire. We call the RV company, who promise to send a tow truck to fix it. They call back to say that he won't be there for at least an hour.

Alisha sticks her head out the window. "Hey, what does RV stand for?"

Ed looks at the sky. "Ruined Vacation." Just then, a bighorn sheep runs across the parking lot, 20 feet away. "Wow!" says Alisha.

"And we wouldn't have seen it if the tire hadn't blown," says Doris. She is determined to make the trip live up to her memories of the last one, which of course she can't really remember.

The tow truck man arrives and changes the tire in less time than it takes Ed to change lanes. Ed shakes the man's hand. "You wouldn't want to come with us to the Grand Canyon, would you?"

Because of the flat, we're two hours behind schedule and won't make it to the RV park where we have a reservation. Doris starts calling random campgrounds in the guidebook. "Hey, they want to know how long our RV is," she calls out.

"About 30 feet too long," yells Ed from the driver's seat.

Doris secures a reservation in an old mining town named Chloride. "The lady says just take the I-40 all the way there."

"But we're not on the I-40," says Ed.

Around 9 p.m., we pull into Chloride, a name that suggests an obsession with hygiene uncorroborated by actual conditions. Phoebe looks out the window dubiously. "This reminds me of that movie where the family in an RV pulls into a little town and the mutants come out at night and eat them."

"It's adorable!" This, from Doris.

We pull into the town's one RV park. The attendant comes over and asks us which side our electrical, water and sewer outlets are on. He calls these "hookups," but we all hear it as "hiccups." The RV park attendant fails to find great humor in this.

After a dinner of refrigerator-baked chicken, it's time for bed. Ed pushes a button, activating a motor that causes one side of the floor to slide outward, doubling the vehicle's width. It's like something James Bond's gadget guy might have come up with after he retired from the spy trade and took up RVing in his dotage.

Ed oversees the sleeping arrangements. Nana and Poppy get the bedroom in the back, which is where the toilet and shower are. This is separated from the main room by a stiff beige curtain that you pull closed behind you, as in a voting booth. The bedroom is minuscule. It would be easier, though possibly a federal offense, to get undressed in a voting booth.

The other two beds are in the kitchen. "For this one," says Lily, "you just drop down the dining table and cut off your feet."

Doris and Alisha take the sofa bed. It appears to be stuck in the shadowy limbo between sofa and bed. Doris appears unconcerned about her impending spinal deformity. "This is the life," she says, speaking directly into her navel.

It's impressive how the RV designers managed to fit it all in, but heaven help you if you have to go to the bathroom—or "go vote," as we now say—after all the beds have been pulled out. Ed offers me advice: "I recommend taking the overland route, bypassing the legs, and then heading west at the overflowing garbage bag. Good luck."

We arrive at the Grand Canyon the next morning. It's beautiful, but it seems empty and lonely and way too quiet. We're all happy to hit the road and get back in each other's faces. RVs are interesting that way.

Yours, Mine & Mine

Our friends Tina and Joe have installed his-and-her sinks. The last time we had dinner there, we all got up with our wineglasses and went in to admire the remodeled bathroom. We stood awhile, sipping our wine and chatting about this and that, as though having cocktails in the bathroom before sitting down to eat was the new thing. It made as much sense to me as individual bathroom sinks did.

"What's up with that?" I said to Ed on the way home. How often does it happen that you are wanting to brush your teeth at precisely the same moment as your spouse, and in such a grave hurry, that you can't wait 40 seconds? Me, I enjoy the goofy intimacy of brushing your teeth together, talking over the day's events in an unintelligible foamy garble. That's what marriage is all about. Isn't it?

"It would be nice to have your own sink," Ed said. "I can't say why."

I launched into one of my tiresome laments about modern life, about how couples don't live like couples anymore, what with his-and-her washbasins and separate phone mailboxes and mattress adjustments and car temperature controls. Couples don't share, because no one's willing to compromise.

Ed was quiet for a moment. "What do we share?"

I thought about this. We share a home e-mail account that neither of us checks or uses or even remembers how to log on to. We share a Netflix account, though it is Ed who manages the film queue. Not long ago, a Jack Black movie featuring the portly actor in a full-body leotard dropped through our mail slot. I ran out the door in my sock-feet, convinced that the mailman had given us a neighbor's envelope. We don't share the same shampoo or breakfast cereal or even toothpaste. I couldn't come up with an answer.

For an experiment in togetherness, I suggested that we share iTunes, the software that allows you to bleed your bank account dry in 99-cent increments—oops, I mean, download songs to create an online music library. Ed already had an iPod, and I had just bought one. (When I was nine or ten, I used my allowance to buy a jack-in-the-box. The toy store clerk, an older woman with dry, permed hair and a grim set to her mouth, not that I harbor any resentment, said, "Aren't you too old for that?" I got to relive that moment right there in the Apple store.)

Our shared music library lasted less than an hour. It was too embarrassing to have Ed know that I'd downloaded a song by, say, Al Stewart. I actually paid the 99 cents, and then, seeing it there on the list between Frank Sinatra and acclaimed avant-garde accordion and glockenspiel trio Tin Hat, I deleted it. And while Ed could skip over my music on the playlist, I had the kind of iPod that chooses songs at random. I'd be bopping along the sidewalk, and "Sweet Home Alabama" would suddenly segue into a neo-klezmer band.

"How could someone not like the Klezmatics?" said Ed. There was an implied "and like Al Stewart" at the end of the question.

"I do like them," I said. "I just would always rather, you know, listen to something else."

Ed made me a separate library file for my music, which he labeled "Out-of-Date Pap," or anyway wanted to. Then he showed me how I could easily copy any of the hundreds of songs in his music library to my own. So I did that. Now there were six songs in my library.

He looked at the list. "Those are the only ones you want?"

I nodded.

"Huh," said Ed. "We're very different, you and I."

We shared that sentiment, and then we went upstairs to spit toothpaste on each other's hands in the sink that, for the moment at least, we share.

Gratuitous Gratuities

Not long ago, a mysterious Christmas card dropped through our mail slot. The envelope was addressed to a man named Raoul, who, I was relatively certain, did not live with us. The envelope wasn't sealed, so I opened it. The inside of the card was blank. My husband explained that the card was both from and to the newspaper deliveryman. His name was apparently Raoul, and Raoul wanted a holiday tip. We were meant to put a check inside the card and then drop the envelope in the mail. When your services are rendered at 4 a.m., you can't simply hang around, clearing your throat like a bellhop. You have to be direct.

So I wrote a nice holiday greeting to this man whom I had never seen or met, this man who, in my imagination, fires the *New York Times* from a howitzer aimed at our front door, causing more noise with mere newsprint than most people manage with sophisticated black market fireworks.

With a start, I realized that perhaps the reason for the

4 a.m. wake-up thonks was not ordinary rudeness but carefully executed spite: I had not tipped Raoul in Christmases past. I honestly hadn't realized I was supposed to. This was the first time he'd used the card tactic. So I got out my checkbook. Somewhere along the line, holiday tipping went from an optional thank-you for a year of services well rendered to a Mafia-style protection racket.

Several days later, I was bringing our garbage bins back from the curb when I noticed an envelope taped to one of the lids. The outside of the envelope said MICKEY. Unless a small person named Mickey had taken up residence in our garbage can and this missive was intended for him, it had to be another tip solicitation, this time from our garbage collector. Unlike Raoul, Mickey hadn't enclosed his own Christmas card from me. In a way, I appreciated the directness. "I know you don't care how merry my Christmas is, and that's fine," the gesture said. "I want $30, or I'll 'forget' to empty your compost bin some hot summer day."

I put a check in the envelope and taped it back to the bin. The next morning, Ed reported that on his way to the gym, he'd noticed that the envelope was gone, though the trash hadn't yet been picked up: "Someone stole Mickey's tip!" Ed concocted a scenario whereby an enterprising colleague of Mickey's had done a late-night sweep of his route, stealing all the tips. He made me call the bank and cancel the check.

But Ed had been wrong. Two weeks later, Mickey left a letter from the bank on our steps. The letter informed Mickey that the check, which he had tried to cash, had been canceled. The following Tuesday morning, Ed ran out with his wallet. "Are you Mickey?"

The man looked at him with scorn. "Mickey is the garbageman. I am the recycling." Not only had Ed insulted this man by insinuating that he was a garbageman, but he had obviously neglected to tip him. Ed ran back inside for more funds. Then he noticed that the driver of the truck had been watching the whole transaction. He peeled off another twenty and looked around, waving bills in the air. "Anyone else?"

Had we consulted the website of the Emily Post Institute, this embarrassing breach of etiquette could have been avoided. Under "trash/recycling collectors" in the institute's Holiday Tipping Guidelines, it says: "$10 to $30 each." You may or may not wish to know that your pet groomer, personal trainer, handyman, hairdresser, mailman and UPS guy all expect a holiday tip.

The Mary Roach Institute has something to say: Enough! People hate tipping. It forces them to make an unpleasant choice between feeling cheap and feeling taken. Americans are nickeled-and-dimed from every direction. Just factor it into your rates and be done with it, I say!

Ed got that look he gets when my true nature breaks through the sweetness-and-light exterior that I prop in place about 20 percent of the time. "Who *are* you?" he said.

I hung my head. "My name is Scrooge. I live in your trash bin."

Color Me Flummoxed

I am a fan of the Sherwin-Williams Company, if only for the crazy audacity of their logo: a giant paint can spilling its contents over Earth. What I want to know is, how did they decide on the color? Painting the earth is a big job. You don't want to do it twice. And red is a bold choice for even the smallest home décor project.

As is yellow. Last year, Ed and I spent 45 minutes flipping through yellow paint chips when we redid our TV room. Seeking something subtle, we went with Peace Yellow. Ed covered two walls. "Whoa!" he said, squinting. It was like living inside Easter. We had failed to observe the Universal Law of Paint Chips: Whatever you choose will be two times brighter, darker and more garish than it looked on the chip.

This time, repainting the guest room, we decided to go with Benjamin Moore. They sell trial paint containers the size of baby-food jars, and, as with baby food, the idea is to smear patches of the stuff all over the walls. This enables you to try the colors out before committing to a full gallon. Off we went to the paint store.

"This is nice," said Ed, holding up a chip of Wyndham Cream. The name was pretty but largely devoid of useful color associations. This bugs me. I like a paint namer who calls it like it is—for instance, the person who came up with Benjamin Moore's American Cheese. Although who in their right mind—not that anybody in the midst of a home décor project is in their right mind—would cover their walls with something suggestive of Velveeta? "Some dogs I know," Ed said. "My nephew. Your friend Clark."

Because Wyndham Cream sounded so lovely, we bought the little jar of it, as well as a jar of Asbury Sand, Crowne Hill Yellow, Hathaway Peach and a couple of others. Only when we got them on the wall did we recognize the colors for what they actually were: Caulk, Jaundice, Band-Aid and Cheap Drugstore Foundation.

Ed had made a huge grid of paint squares on the wall. The guest room looked like *The Hollywood Squares*. We stared at the grid for a long time. "Paul Lynde isn't that bad," I said.

"I could live with Charo," said Ed.

After a half hour of this, we had to accept the fact that we didn't care for any of them. We had just spent more money on sample-sized jars of paint than we'd spent on the wasted gallon of Peace Yellow. We'd been taken by the names, by peaches that turned out to be first aid supplies. This is the surprising thing about people who name paint colors: Many are color-blind. What else can explain why Bonfire is dark red or Greenfield Pumpkin is brown? Ed pointed out that I have never visited Greenfield, nor looked upon its winter squashes. "You don't know, really," he said. "Could be something in the water there."

If only to get away from the depressing home décor scenario playing itself out in the guest room, I went downstairs and Googled *pumpkin* and *Greenfield*. I couldn't find an image of a Greenfield pumpkin, but I did find a news item headlined "Pumpkin Launcher Accident in Greenfield, New Hampshire." The operator of a catapult built for pumpkin-chuckin' contests was knocked out when the device hit him on the chin.

"What color is the pumpkin launcher?" Ed asked. Lo and behold, it was brown. Ed surmised that *Greenfield Pumpkin* was a Benjamin Moore typo and that the person who named it had actually called it Greenfield Pumpkin Launcher.

"You know," said Ed, looking at the chip, "it's kind of nice."

"Uh-huh," I said. "Matches the rug."

And so we went with Greenfield Pumpkin Launcher.

Change Is Not Good

A man's front pants pocket is a one-way portal to his dresser top. Coins go in, but they are never pulled back out and spent. I have seen my husband, Ed, receive 97 cents in change, dump it all in his pocket and then pull a dollar bill out for the tip jar. This appears to be a near-universal male trait. We have all seen the news stories of elderly men buried under the rubble when the bedroom floor finally collapses under the weight of 55 years of pocket change.

The Bank of Ed resides in empty sauerkraut jars and assorted broken crockery that has found a second career in finance. "Coins are heavy, but at least they're dry," the mug with no handle will say to the chipped cereal bowl.

One year, for his birthday, I got Ed a noisy, battery-powered machine to roll his coins. Unfortunately, this particular machine used special rolls that you had to send away for. By the time your special rolls arrived in the mail, your wife and children would have long ago jammed the machine by feeding it buttons and subway tokens just to see what happened.

Most men's coins are rolled by a noisy, irritation-powered machine called a wife. I spent the better part of a Thursday evening rolling two years' worth of Ed's coins the old-fashioned way. On Saturday we loaded up two canvas tote bags full of money and pushed our way through the bank's front doors, like robbers in reverse. We began piling the rolls on the narrow shelf in front of the teller's window, where the missing and nonfunctional ballpoint pens live. The teller stopped us. "You'll need to write your name and full 16-digit bank account number on each of those rolls," she said. I obviously looked like the kind of person who pads her coin rolls with buttons and subway tokens. Just to see what happens.

A sympathetic woman who had been in line behind us said that the Lucky supermarket nearby had an automatic change-counting machine. While we drove there, I gently probed Ed about his change-hoarding habits. Why couldn't he spend the coins as he got them? He explained that he set them aside on purpose, so that at the end of the year, he'd have a couple hundred dollars to do something fun with.

"Like driving coins down to Lucky?"

"Something like that."

On the pavement outside Lucky, a workman was unloading pallets of canned chicken broth. There were hundreds upon hundreds of cans, stacked as high as the workman's head. It was what the top of Ed's dresser would have looked like if stores gave you chicken broth instead of coins for change.

On the front of the Coinstar machine was a sticker informing us that an 8.9 percent "counting fee" would be subtracted from our total unless we chose to receive gift cards—for Amazon.com, Starbucks, iTunes, Eddie Bauer—instead of cash. I was surprised to see iTunes on there because I think of coin rolling and change exchanging as a pastime of the middle-aged and elderly. I picture young people just throwing their change away.

In case there was any question as to whether you'd count us among the young or the middle-aged and elderly, Ed chose Eddie Bauer.

We began pouring handfuls of coins into the basket. "Can we trust it?" I said. "How do we know it's not skimming?"

Not that I would know anything about skimming. The five or six dollars a week that I take from Ed's coin stash for bus fare and parking meters is not skimmed. It's a "rolling fee."

The machine tallied up 5,288 coins. We now own a slip of paper entitling us to $403 in Eddie Bauer store credit, which will spend its days atop Ed's dresser, alongside the broken mugs and cereal bowls and pallets of chicken broth.

One Good Tern . . .

Late one fall afternoon, a flock of cedar waxwings descended on our backyard. I get excited by a bird with a crest. They're the royalty, the showstoppers. I barreled into the den to get my binoculars. Ed was watching the game. "Cedar waxwings!" I yelled.

"St. Louis Cardinals!" Ed yelled back.

I paused in the doorway. "Have you ever even seen a cedar waxwing?"

"It's a bird," said Ed. "I've seen birds. They fly, they sing a little ditty."

I was raised by bird-watchers. My mother filled bird feeders and cadged hunks of suet from the A&P butchers to hang on trees for the woodpeckers. At a young age, I learned the simple satisfaction of identifying a new bird all by myself and then making the decisive check mark on the life list in the back of the bird guide. No one notices birds in my husband's family. They view bird-watching as a sort of quaint, perplexing mental illness. I have heard Ed refer to birders as people who pull their pants up a little too high.

When I first went to Florida with Ed and his daughters to visit his parents, I tried to drag everyone out to the Wakodahatchee Wetlands to see the storks and ibises. *Wakodahatchee* is a native word meaning "swamp that serves as a major mosquito breeding ground for the greater South Florida region."

"Do we have to go?" Lily would say.

"It stinks there," Phoebe would chime in.

I once dragged them out to the Everglades in search of the roseate spoonbill, a large storklike item with a bald green head and a long spatulate beak.

"Imagine trying to eat with no hands," I said to Lily and Phoebe, hoping to spark their interest. "Imagine trying to pick up a fish with a set of mixing spoons that have been stuck to your face."

Phoebe swatted a mosquito. "Imagine getting the hell out of here."

Lily yawned. "Imagine going back to Nana's and lying out by the pool."

The late-afternoon sun had deepened the waxwings' colors. The last quarter inch of a waxwing's tail feathers is bright yellow, as though it had been dipped in paint. I don't know why this should thrill me so, but it does. "Are you sure you don't want to come see them?" I said to Ed. He was sure. I told him birding would be good for him. He could use another active hobby, something that gets him out into nature.

"That's true," said Ed's friend Brian, who was watching the game with him. "Like me. I'm taking up golf."

Ed frowned. "I'm taking up space."

I recently bought a software program called Handheld Birds—a bird guide with birdcall audio files and checklists built in—which can be loaded onto a PalmPilot. While it was nice to have the birdcalls with me in the field, the appeal of a handheld device, for me, was more basic: Fewer people would peg me as a birder and think derisive thoughts about me. Instead, they'd think, *There's a successful businesswoman checking her many pressing engagements while standing in the woods at 6 a.m. on a Saturday.*

I soon went back to my bird guide. If I'm trying to identify, say, a new tern species, I need to see all the terns at once, laid out for comparison on a page or two. The handheld limits you to viewing one species at a time, though it does provide a lot more information on each of those species. You can zoom in on a blowup of the bird with its distinctive features pointed out—the blue bill of the ruddy duck, the white underpants of the pigeon guillemot. It's possible I misread this and that what it says is "white underparts." But I prefer to picture the guillemot standing out on the rocks in a pair of white underpants, no doubt pulled up just a little too high.

Talking the Walk

It began, as most backpacking trips do, in a ranger station. The ranger was explaining to Ed and me that we would need a bear bag. This is a special food bag that you hang over the end of a tree branch so the bears don't come into your tent and don't get into your food. "Bears are too heavy," the ranger said, "to go out on a limb."

"Lot of bears up there this time of year?" asked Ed.

His tone was calm, conversational even, but I, unlike the bears, will go out on a limb and say that Ed was uncomfortable with the bear concept. As was I.

"No bears." The ranger narrowed his gaze. "Marmots."

It was as close as a park ranger gets to cursing. The marmot, according to one of the handouts he gave us, "will eat virtually anything" and will "chew through your pack to get food."

I can never get a good fix on the forest ranger personality: calm and carefree—or quietly desperate? Most likely it's something of a mix. In exchange for being able to live in places where the rest of us go for vacation, they are forced to wear bulky uniforms and have tedious conversations about permit fees and wilderness etiquette.

Ed stood at the rack of free informational handouts, carefully taking one of each. One had a crude trail map of this particular patch of the Sierras, leading him to believe we could make do without a real map. It was the sort of decision that causes friends and neighbors to shake their heads sadly: *To think they lost their lives for six dollars.*

Consulting our crude map, we chose a trail that appeared to be a reasonable day's hike for middle-aged people bearing 25-pound packs. That is to say, a short one. In the end, the trail turned out to be five miles long with a 2,000-foot elevation gain.

At a waterfall we believed to be the halfway point, we stopped for lunch. It was well before noon, but when Ed is hungry, it is best to address the matter. He will chew through your pack to get food. Besides, we were beat. The rushing water was barely audible over the sound of our panting.

"Beautiful spot," I wheezed.

"Yup," said Ed, massaging his knee. "We should come here when we're ten years younger."

Because we had only cheese and crackers and peanut butter for lunch, it was over dismayingly soon. Backpacking is an excellent dieting activity, as the normal desire to overeat is outweighed by the desire to keep one's pack light.

Back on the trail, we passed an old stone cabin. A plaque informed us that it had belonged to the actor Lon Chaney. Ed wondered aloud how Chaney had managed to haul the stones all this way into the woods.

"Maybe that's how he became a hunchback," I offered.

Ed ignored me. He took out the map. "If the cabin is here," he said, "then we're barely a third of the way."

We were silent for a moment, contemplating the distance ahead. A man on a horse passed us. Behind him were two more horses, carrying the backpacks of a group of hikers who had sped past us some time ago. "Remind me," I said. "Why is it that we didn't do that?"

A few hours later, we rounded a bend, and there below us was the answer to my question: a glacial lake, aqua-hued and sprinkled with shimmering spots of sun. No one else was around. We set up the tent and played Scrabble. As the sky turned pink, Ed cooked up some dehydrated beans and instant rice, which we ate with cilantro and hot sauce from a teeny plastic bottle that would later leak all over the camp towel.

It's possible the food would have tasted just as good if horses had carried our packs—but I doubt it.

About the Author

Mary Roach is the author of *Gulp: Adventures on the Alimentary Canal*. Her previous works include *Stiff: The Curious Lives of Human Cadavers*; *Spook: Science Tackles the Afterlife*; *Bonk: The Curious Coupling of Science and Sex*; and *Packing for Mars: The Curious Science of Life in the Void*. Her essays have appeared in *Vogue*, *GQ*, *National Geographic*, and *Wired*.